The

Little WordPerfect for Windows Book

Kay Yarborough Nelson

Peachpit Press
Berkeley, California

The Little WordPerfect for Windows Book
Kay Yarborough Nelson

Peachpit Press, Inc.
2414 Sixth St.
Berkeley, CA 94710
(510) 548-4393
(510) 548-5591 (fax)

Copyright © 1992 by Kay Yarborough Nelson

Cover design:Ted Mader + Associates (TMA)

ISBN 0-938151-44-4

0 9 8 7 6 5 4 3 2 1
Printed and bound in the United States of America

Contents

Chapter 10: WordPerfect and Windows   95

Chapter 11: Printing   105

Introduction

This *Little* book isn't just for beginners. It's for the vast majority of WordPerfect for Windows users: you who just want to see how to do something without reading a whole lot of detail about it or working through a tedious exercise that probably isn't related to what you're doing anyway. It won't cover everything that WordPerfect can do, or it would be a *big* book. But you probably don't want to do everything that the program can, and if there are specialized and arcane things you need to do, there are lots of other sources of information about WordPerfect, including its great Help facility. This book will get you through most things, and then some.

It's also a great book for those of you who are making the switch to upgrade from WordPerfect DOS to WordPerfect for Windows, since I spend a lot of time pointing out the differences between what you already know and what's different in the Windows version. Marginal tips also help point out topics that upgraders will be especially interested in.

Upgrading from WordPerfect DOS?

It's an excellent choice for those of you who are just starting out in Windows and WordPerfect, too, since it doesn't make any assumptions that you already know what the weird key combinations do or the tricks for working with Windows. There's a whole beginning chapter on the keyboard and the mouse, and another chapter devoted entirely to working with Windows.

New to Windows?

The Fast Track   If you've used Windows, WordPerfect, or another word processing program before, you shouldn't get bogged down by "easy" topics in this book, though. In fact, you'll find chapters that cover formatting tricks and keyboard shortcuts that will get you going right away. Chapter 6, "State Your Preferences," will get you started customizing your copy of WordPerfect for Windows to work the way that you want it to.

And if you're interested in some of WordPerfect's more sophisticated techniques like creating tables, setting text in columns, editing graphics, creating links between documents, and recording simple macros, and so forth, you'll find that their basics are covered here, too. You'll be surprised at how easy these "hard" features are to use.

Absolute Beginner?   If you're really, really beginning and you've never used a word processing program before, here, in a nutshell, are the secrets that lots of folks sit all day in a seminar to discover:

- When you get to the end of a line (the edge of your screen), don't press Enter (that big funny-looking key that's shaped like a backward L). Just keep on typing. The words will automatically wrap to the next line, and your position in the line will be indicated by a small flashing underline called the **cursor.** Press Enter only when you want to start a new paragraph. If you want to insert a blank line, press Enter *twice*.

- Nothing is final until you say so. In other words, what you see on the screen isn't permanent until you save it. In WordPerfect for Windows, this means choosing Save from the File menu or button bar, or pressing Shift and F3 at the same time. This works both to your advantage and to your disadvantage. The bad news first: If you don't save your work, you'll lose it when you turn off your computer or if the lights go out. But saving (or not saving) can also work to your advantage: if you mess up a document, you can just get its previously saved version back by closing the messed-up version without saving it. So follow this rule of thumb: *save each time you do some work that you don't want to lose*. WordPerfect thoughtfully provides an automatic backup feature that will save for you even if you forget to.

These two rules are your basic Introduction to Word Processing. Think of how much money and time you've saved already!

This is a little book to keep next to your computer and look up whatever you happen to need. It's more than an instant reference, because it tells you the best, fastest way to do things instead of giving you all the alternate ways of carrying out a task. And sometimes there may be five or six ways to do any one thing, if you count the keyboard shortcuts, the mnemonics, the function keys, the menus, the button bar, the ruler bar, the mouse...! So enjoy it. I enjoyed writing it. This is a great program.

Enjoy!

The Keyboard and the Mouse

1

A chapter of import to rank beginners and users of other word processing programs alike, including WordPerfect DOS.

Some of the most important things you need to know about WordPerfect for Windows aren't about the program at all. They're about using the keyboard and the mouse. These are the two ways you communicate with the program and tell it what you want it to do. And yes, you really do need a mouse, because there are some things in Word-Perfect for Windows, like using the button bar and the ruler, that just can't be done without one.

Your Keyboard

If you've never used WordPerfect before, you may not be aware that it assigns different functions to some of the keys on the keyboard. Follow along as we review some of those, even if you've used other programs before. If you're an old hand at DOS WordPerfect, you should be aware that WordPerfect for Windows (using the default keyboard) uses Windows' interpretation for keys, not the ones you're used to (see Chapter 12, "Shortcuts," for more about all sorts of shortcuts you can take.)

Those Strange Keys

There are some pretty bewildering keys on a computer keyboard. If it gets much more complex, it'll look like an instrument panel on a plane. Here's a quick rundown of what's where, showing the main part of the keyboard. Your keyboard may be a bit different from this one. You'll also have special keys called **function keys** either on the left side of your keyboard or at the top. Some keyboards like the Northgate OmniKey even have them in both places. We'll get to those in a minute.

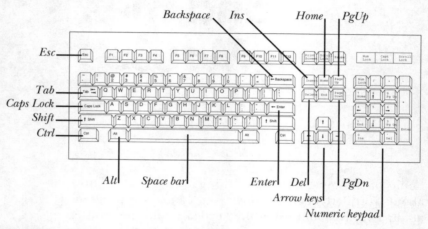

The Enter Key The most basic key is the Enter key. It's that odd-shaped one on the right of the alphabet keys. As you saw earlier, you use it to end a paragraph or insert a blank line. In WordPerfect, you also use it to confirm a choice you've made from a menu. Instead of clicking OK or Yes or No, you can just press the Enter key to accept the choice WordPerfect is giving you, the one that's in a shaded box.

Tab The Tab key is probably the second most important. It's at the other end of the alphabet keys, over near the Q. It has two arrows on it. If you're lucky, it's labeled "Tab," because otherwise you might never figure out what those arrows mean. Pressing Tab indents your line one tab stop (half an inch, if you haven't changed WordPerfect's default settings). If you want your paragraphs indented, this is the key to press.

To go back one tab stop, press Shift+Tab. By the way, in this book, this notation (with the plus sign) means "press Shift and Tab at the same time." That's the way the Windows and WordPerfect manuals do it, too. If you see "press Home Home" it means "press Home once and then press Home again."

The Shift key is like the Shift key on a typewriter: pressing it gets you uppercase characters. If you want to type in ALL CAPS for a while, you can press the Caps Lock key instead of holding the Shift key down. To turn off Caps Lock, press Caps Lock again. By the way, it's considered a sign of computer illiteracy if you type very much with the Caps Lock key down, so use it sparingly. Just be aware that it's there.

Shift

There's another use for the Shift key in WordPerfect, and that's to issue commands as keyboard shortcuts. For instance, you can press Shift+Del to cut selected text and Shift+Ins to paste it. You'll see lots of these keyboard shortcuts in this book.

To correct mistakes, you use the Backspace and Del keys. The Backspace key is above the Enter key, and it has a left-pointing arrow on it. The Del key is over on the far right of your keyboard, labeled "Del." On some keyboards, there's another Delete key above the arrow keys. Both Backspace and Del keys delete characters, but they do it in slightly different ways:

Backspace and Del

- The Backspace key deletes the character that's to the left of the insertion point (the blinking I-beam that indicates where text will appear in the document as you type).

- The Del key deletes the character the insertion point's on.

The Insert key (it's usually next to the Del key) switches you into Typeover mode. Insert mode is the factory setting, also called the "default" setting. In Insert mode, the characters that you type appear where the insertion point is and don't erase other characters. In Typeover mode, what you type replaces characters that are already there. You probably won't use Typeover much unless you're correcting columns of numbers, in which case it's pretty handy. That's the only time I ever use it.

Insert

By the way, the Insert key, like Caps Lock, is what's called a **toggle:** pressing it once turns the feature on, and pressing it again turns it off.

Num Lock

The Num Lock key is at the top of what's called the **numeric keypad**, over on the right of your keyboard. Use it if you're entering a lot of numbers, because it's faster to type numbers from the numeric keypad than to type them from the number keys at the top of the keyboard. There's usually a little raised dot on the central 5 key so that touch typists can use the numeric keypad as a 10-key entry pad.

▶ **Tip:** *There are usually Insert and Del keys on the numeric keypad, too.*

On many computers, the Num Lock key comes on automatically when you start your computer. In WordPerfect you can use that numeric keypad for lots of other, more useful things like moving through your document. The 4, 8, 6, and 2 keys work like arrow keys, and PgUp and PgDn move you up and down one screen. So having Num Lock on all the time can get irritating. You might want to reach over there now and press it to turn it off, if it's on. There's usually a lighted indicator that tells you when it's on.

The Arrow Keys

To the left of the numeric keypad is a small triangular block of arrow keys. These move you left or right one character at a time, or up or down one line at a time, as you might expect.

Esc

WordPerfect for Windows uses the Esc key (over on the left of the chatacter keys, above the Tab key) as a Cancel key to cancel whatever you've decided against doing. If you're in a dialog box, pressing Esc exits you from the box without making any choices, even if you've changed things in the box. If you're in a menu, pressing Esc backs you up to the next highest level of menus. If you're in the main menu, you leave the menu system and return to your document when you press Esc.

▶ **Tip:** *If you're upgrading from WordPerfect DOS, be aware that Cancel is no longer F1. Help is F1 now.*

By the way, if you're used to WordPerfect DOS, you'll probably try to use the F1 key as the Cancel key. Not any more. F1 is the Help key in WordPerfect for Windows, even if you're using the optional DOS-style keyboard. (You can switch keyboards from the Windows-style keyboard to the WordPerfect DOS-style keyboard by using the Preferences menu, as you'll see in Chapter 6, "State Your Preferences.")

WordPerfect for Windows makes good use of the Ctrl key. By itself, it doesn't do anything. But pressed along with other keys, it does all sorts of things. You can use it for many keyboard shortcuts. Here's a sample:

Ctrl+X	Cut
Ctrl+C	Copy
Ctrl+V	Paste
Ctrl+B	Bold
Ctrl+I	Italics
Ctrl+N	Normal
Ctrl+G	Go To
Ctrl-F	Justify Full
Ctrl+P	Print

There are lots of other keyboard shortcuts. Some use the Shift and Ctrl keys along with other key combinations. You'll see many of them in this book as we go along.

These keys do pretty much what you'd expect: move you forward or backward through your document. On some keyboards, you get two sets of them: one above the arrow keys and another on the numeric keypad.

In WordPerfect for Windows, the End key gets a good workout. Pressing End takes you to the end of the line you're on. Pressing Ctrl and End together takes you to the end of your document. Pressing Shift+End extends a selection to the end of the line. And there are several more End key combinations, too. We'll take a look at them when we talk about specfic tasks later.

In WordPerfect for Windows, pressing Ctrl and Home at the same time takes you to the beginning of your document. Otherwise the Home key doesn't do much. But if you're using the DOS-style keyboard, you'll find that the Home key works pretty much the way it did in WordPerfect DOS.

Ctrl

▶ **Tip:** *Upgraders, these new Ctrl key shortcuts are great. They're easier to remember than the Windows-style shortcuts, if you're not used to Windows.*

Page Up, Page Down

End

▶ **Tip:** *If you're coming to WordPerfect from WordPerfect DOS, be warned that the End key doesn't always work the way you expect it to, even if you're using the optional DOS-style keyboard.*

Home

▶ **Tip:** *If you're upgrading from WordPerfect DOS, be aware that the Home key doesn't work the way you'll expect it to.*

On the DOS-style keyboard, the Home key works as a modifier key for a lot of things. Pressing Home by itself doesn't do anything, but when you press Home first and then use another key, things really happen. Think of Home as meaning "really." Here's how it works:

- Home Left arrow takes you to the beginning of the line (really left)

- Home Right arrow takes you to the end of the line (really right)

- Home Up arrow takes you to the top of your screen

- Home Down arrow takes you to the bottom of your screen

- Home Home Up arrow takes you to the beginning of your document (really really up)

- Home Home Down arrow takes you to the end of your document (really really down)

- And Home Home Home Up arrow takes you to the really really really beginning of your document, before any invisible formatting codes that you can't normally see.

Don't worry about all these ways of moving through your document for now. Just remember that if you're upgrading, don't expect the Home key to work the way you're used to unless you switch to the other keyboard.

Other keys There are a lot of other keys on your keyboard. Some of them you'll use in WordPerfect and some of them you won't. WordPerfect doesn't have any use for Scroll Lock or Pause, for example. But it does use the function keys.

The Function Keys The function keys on the left of your keyboard, or maybe at the top, depending on which kind of keyboard you have, are the key to giving WordPerfect commands if you don't use the menus. For a long time, using these function keys was the only way to give WordPerfect commands, which is the reason a lot of folks found WordPerfect hard to use. The keys F1 through F10 have one meaning if they're pressed by themselves, another meaning if you press Ctrl and a function key, a third meaning if you press Shift and a function key, and a fourth meaning if you press Alt and a function key. In WordPerfect for Windows, they have a fifth meaning if you press Ctrl and Shift and a function key, and a sixth if you press Alt and Shift and a function key. Wow. That's why WordPerfect Corporation supplies you with a template showing all these combinations.

If you've lost your template, or if the cat has batted it into the fourth dimension, you can see on the screen the template for both the Windows-style keyboard (it's called the CUA keyboard, for Common User Access) and the DOS-style keyboard. Just choose Keyboards from the Help menu (or press F1, which gets you Help, too).

▶ **Tip:** *Lost your template? Choose Keyboards from the Help menu*

Keyboard Tricks

If there's a particularly neat shortcut you can use through the keyboard, I'll tell you about it. Sometimes it's better to use the keyboard, and sometimes it's better to use a mouse. Using a mouse is great for some things, like selecting text, but not so hot for others, when you want to keep your hands on the keyboard and not have to reach for the mouse for just one click.

The Mouse

Since you're using Windows, you must have a mouse. You can use a mouse to do almost everything in WordPerfect for Windows except type text for you. In fact, there are some features of WordPerfect for Windows that you can't even use at all if you don't have a mouse.

There are all sorts of things you can do with a mouse. For example, you can:

- Move and size windows
- Select text so that you can copy it, cut it, paste it, check its spelling, change its font, or do many other different things to it
- Choose commands
- Make selections from dialog boxes
- Move icons
- Move text to a new location

- Resize graphics
- Select buttons from the button bar
- Move through your document via the scroll bar

If you haven't used a mouse before, you'll be amazed at all the different things you can do with it. Want to try a few?

First, start WordPerfect and get some text on your screen. Then move the mouse on your desktop and see how the pointer moves on the screen. Now, here's the real mouse secret; this is another one they don't often tell you. *You can pick the mouse up and the pointer doesn't disappear.* So it's easy to reposition the mouse pointer without knocking your teacup over. Just pick the mouse up and move it.

Now press the left mouse button and drag the mouse across some text that's on the screen. You'll see highlighting appear over it. When text is highlighted, it's selected. When it's selected, you can do all the things listed above to it, like cutting, copying, and pasting it.

To select just one word, put the mouse pointer on it and double-click with the left mouse button (click twice rapidly). To select the sentence that the word's in, click three times, or triple-click. To extend a selection without dragging the mouse, click at the beginning of the text you want to select, press the Shift key, and then click at the end of the text. Try these out until you and your hand get the idea.

Using a mouse may be a little awkward at first if you're not used to it. Someone told me this trick that can speed up the learning process: use the mouse in your *other* hand for a bit. If you're right-handed, try it in your left hand for a while. If you're left-handed, try it in your right hand. Then, when you switch back to your "right" hand, the mouse will feel a lot more comfortable.

You can customize how your mouse "feels" in your hand. To customize how your mouse works, you don't use WordPerfect, though. You use the Windows Control Panel and choose the Mouse icon. If you're left-handed, you can make your mouse a left-handed mouse, too (a southpaw?), by switching the effects of the left and right mouse buttons. You can also change the tracking speed, which is the rate that the mouse pointer moves across the screen as you move it on your real desktop. And you can change the double-click rate from slower to faster, which is important because making multiple clicks are a basic part of using a mouse with WordPerfect.

As you've seen, in WordPerfect for Windows, you can just double-click on a word to select it or triple-click to select a sentence. You can also click four times (I just can't bear to say "quadruple-click") to select a paragraph. These are all really handy shortcuts, so be sure to set a click rate you're comfortable with. If your double-clicks (or triple-clicks, or four clicks) are being interpreted as single clicks, go change the mouse's double-click speed in Windows.

Now that you've been introduced to the basics of the keyboard and the mouse, we can get on with the tour of WordPerfect for Windows in the next chapter.

On with the Show

A Guided Tour

The famous fifty-cent tour provided with this book.

In this chapter we'll take a quick guided tour of WordPerfect for Windows. If you haven't already got WordPerfect running on your computer, start it now so that you can follow along. To start WordPerfect, start Windows and then double-click on the WordPerfect icon in the WordPerfect program group.

Your screen will look very much like the one shown here. If you don't see the button bar and the ruler, choose them from the View menu.

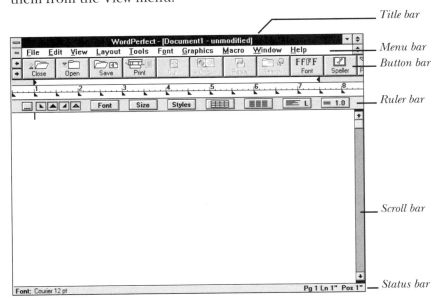

Title bar

Menu bar

Button bar

Ruler bar

Scroll bar

Status bar

The Title Bar   Across the very top of the screen is the **title bar,** which indicates that you're working in WordPerfect and gives the name of the document you're working on. If you haven't saved the document yet, it'll say "unmodified."

The Menu Bar   Underneath the title bar is the **menu bar.** If you click on any one of these menu names with the mouse, or press Alt and type the underlined letter in the menu's name, the menu appears. We'll take a closer look at menus in a minute.

The Button Bar   Under the menu bar is the **button bar.** This is an alternate way to use WordPerfect commands by clicking on icons instead of using the menus. The program comes with a predefined button bar that has the most commonly used commands, like Open and Close and so forth. You can choose other specialized button bars for editing graphics, tables, and equations, and you can create your own button bars for the tasks you do most often, too (see Chapter 7, "The Fabulous Button Bar.")

The Status Bar   At the bottom of the window is the **status bar,** which indicates on the left what font you're using and its point size, and on the right shows what page you're on, what line you're on, and the distance of the **insertion point** (the blinking I-beam cursor) from the left margin. You can change the units of measure from the default of inches to points, centimeters, or 1200ths of an inch (for fine-tuning things like placing graphics) by using the Preferences menu (it's on the File menu).

▶ **Tip:** *Don't confuse the mouse pointer with the insertion point. You can move the insertion point by moving the mouse pointer and clicking in text.*

The status bar will also give you a message about what items on the menus are for as you use the pull-down menus.

The Scroll Bar   At the right of the window is the **scroll bar.** You can use it for moving quickly through your documents. Just drag the scroll box down; then release the mouse button. This takes you toward the end of the document that's displayed in the window. To go toward the beginning of the document, drag the box up and release the mouse button.

One way to move quickly through a long document is to click in the scroll bar at just about the place you want to go to. If you click in the middle of the document, you'll go to about the middle of the document. Clicking at the top of the scroll bar takes you to the top of the document.

You can also click on the small arrows at either end of the scroll bar to scroll up or down one line at a time.

There's another scroll bar that you can use, if you choose Display from the Preferences menu and click Display Horizontal Scroll Bar. Normally you probably won't need it, but if the text on your screen is wider than the screen can display (if you have a big spreadsheet or a lot of columns, for example), you may want to use this horizontal scroll bar, too.

There are other, usually faster, ways to move through your document instead of using the scroll bars, as you'll see in Chapter 12, "Shortcuts."

The Ruler

The ruler's not usually visible, but you may want to keep it displayed because you can do so many things with it. For example, you can

- Set tabs
- Change the fonts and the font size
- Change justification
- Create and edit tables
- Create and edit columns
- Change line spacing
- Change left and right margins and column margins, too
- Use Styles

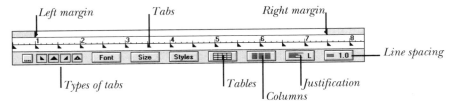

Press Alt+Shift+F3 to show and hide the ruler, or choose Ruler from the View menu.

You can click once on most of the ruler's icons, or drag them (like the tab and margin markers) to change things from the ruler. *Double*-clicking on most of these icons will bring up a dialog box.

Reveal Codes

Another thing that's not normally visible on your screen is the Reveal Codes window. This is the window that shows all the invisible formatting codes that WordPerfect is putting in as you create your document. The lower window shows the same text that you can see in the upper window, except that it's in draft mode and shows the formatting codes, too. For example, [HRrt] indicates a hard return, and so on.

Click here or here and drag to open the Reveal Codes window

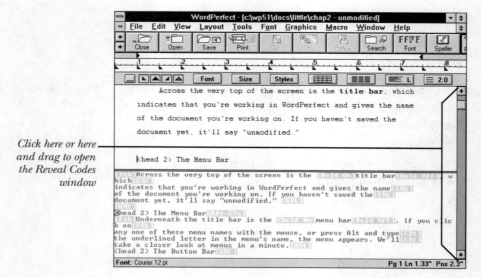

Pressing Alt+F3 will open the Reveal Codes window, or you can choose it from the View menu. There's an even faster way to open it, too: click just above the top or bottom of the scroll bar. The mouse pointer will change shape, a line will appear, and you can drag it to open the Reveal Codes window to any size you like. You can also make a button for Reveal Codes if you'd prefer to open its window by clicking on an icon; Chapter 7, "The Fabulous Button Bar," will show you how.

Once the Reveal Codes window is open, you can edit text in it just as you do in the main document window. Just click in it with the mouse to move the insertion point to a different place.

To close the Reveal Codes window once you're viewing it, just drag its line down off the screen. You can also press Alt+F3 again or choose Reveal Codes again from the View menu.

To set the colors that the Reveal Codes window displays, use the Preferences menu and choose Display. Reveal Codes always appears in draft mode, so don't expect to be able to see the font you're using there.

Keep the following rule in mind, and you'll save yourself a lot of trouble: *If things aren't appearing on the screen like you think they ought to, check the Reveal Codes window.* It's probably an incorrect formatting code that's causing the problem.

You may want to make yourself a button for displaying both the ruler and the Reveal Codes window.

The Minimize, Maximize, and Restore Icons

The **Maximize** and **Minimize** icons let you reduce a program or document down to icon size and then blow it up again to full-screen size. There are two sets of them, one for WordPerfect (the one on top) and one for the document that's open.

- If you click on the program's Minimize icon, you'll make the whole WordPerfect program into an icon on your Windows desktop. This is useful if you're temporarily going to another program but you want to keep WordPerfect in memory without cluttering your screen with lots of open documents.

- You can click on the document's Minimize icon to minimize just the document while you continue to work in WordPerfect or in another program.

When something's minimized, it's still in memory, ready to work with again as soon as you double-click on it. Once you've used the Speller, minimize it and keep it that way, because you can get it back again quickly. Minimizing the File Manager and the Thesaurus speeds up access to them, too. If you're planning to visit the File Manager or use the

▶ **Tip:** *Minimize the Speller for faster access instead of closing it.*

Thesaurus more than once, minimize them into icons; then resize your document window so that you can see their icons at the bottom of the screen.

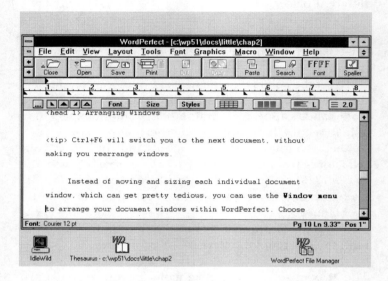

If a window's already maximized (as big as it can get), you'll see a double-headed **Restore** icon instead of a Minimize icon.

- Clicking on the program's Restore icon makes WordPerfect into a medium-sized window. This is handy if you want to be able to see part of your Windows desktop to switch to a different program, use the Control Panel, or go out to the WordPerfect File Manager once you've started it and minimized it (more about the File Manager, Chapter 14).

- Clicking on the document's Restore icon makes the document into a medium-sized window. Why would you want to do this? Well, if you're cutting and pasting text or graphics between two documents, it's handy to be able to see into each of them, so you can make their windows medium-sized and each one won't fill up the whole screen. (As a matter of fact, you can have as many as *nine* documents open in WordPerfect for Windows, if you've got enough memory.)

Minimize | Maximize

Restore

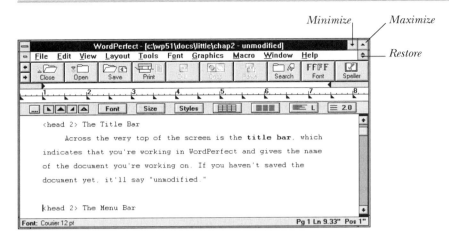

Sizing Windows

Once a document's been shrunk to medium size, you click the Restore button again to make it fill the screen. The button will have only one arrowhead on it, this time pointing upward to indicate that bigger is the only way to go.

You can change the size of a window another way, too: by dragging on its corners. The trick here is to first *make the window small enough to see the corners.* If the window's full-screen size, click the Restore button make it smaller. Then click on the lower-right corner and drag the corner inward (to make the window smaller) or outward (to make it larger).

To reposition a window on the screen, drag it by its title bar. Release the mouse button when you've got the window where you want it.

▶ **Tip:** *You can move any window that has a title bar, like a Speller window.*

The Control Menu

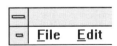

The tiny icons in the upper-left corner of the screen bring upthe **Control menus.** There's one for WordPerfect itself (on the top) and another one for each document (on the bottom). You can click on this icon to bring up a menu that lets you move and resize windows, too, but it's usually faster to do it the other way, by using the icons on the right.

The only things I find that the Control menu is useful for are (1) closing a document and (2) exiting WordPerfect.

▶ **Tip:** *By the way, double-clicking on the Program Manager's Control icon is a quick way to exit Windows.*

- To close a document, double-click on the document Control menu icon, the one with the smaller slit. If you haven't saved the document, you'll get a chance to.

- To exit WordPerfect and return to Windows, just double-click on the Control menu icon on the top (the one with the larger slit) to exit WordPerfect and return to the Program Manager.

▶ **Tip:** *To go out to Windows temporarily (to use a control panel or something), click on WordPerfect's Restore icon (the double-headed one). Then you can click on the Windows desktop to make it active.*

The other choices on the Control menu, in my opinion, are all easier to do with keyboard shortcuts so that you don't have to move the mouse pointer to the left side of the screen. For example, there's a useful Next command on the document Control menu that lets you switch between your WordPerfect documents. It's much faster to press Ctrl+F6 to cycle through your open documents than to slide the mouse pointer over to the left and use the icon.

Arranging Windows

▶ **Tip:** *Ctrl+F6 will switch you to the next document, without making you rearrange windows.*

Instead of moving and sizing each individual document window, which can get pretty tedious, you can use the **Window menu** to arrange your document windows within WordPerfect. Choose **Cascade** to see your documents arranged like a deck of cards, with only their title bars showing. Choose **Tile** to see each document in a tiny window of its own. The active window's always the one with the dark title bar.

Cascading windows

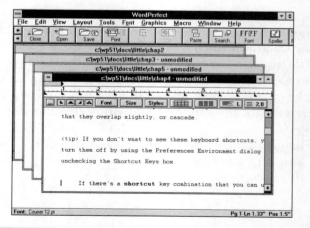

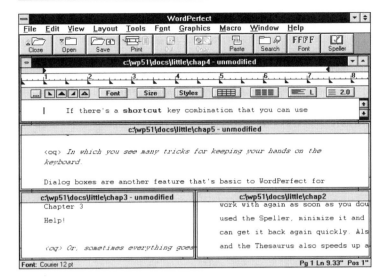

Tiling windows is useful if you're cutting and pasting or copying between documents because you can see a bit of what's in each window. But if you're working on a large number of documents and you only need to be in one window at a time, choose Cascade. You'll still be able to switch between them by just clicking in the title bar of the one you want to go to.

The Window menu

The Window menu lists all the documents you've got open, and you can just click on the name of the document you want to switch to. This is a very handy way to switch if you've got a lot of documents open, because you can just click on the one you want and go straight to it. But if you find that you're switching a lot, you'll probably also find that cascading the windows is a quick way to be able to switch quickly.

Retrieving and Saving Documents

So now that you've seen the basic "knobs" on WordPerfect's instrument panel, you're still faced with that pretty much blank screen. There are two basic things you can do in a document window:

▶ **Tip:** *There's a difference between Open and Retrieve: Retrieve brings the document you select into the document you're already working with.*

- Start typing text to create a new document.
- Open a document you've already created.

To open a document that already exists, you use the File menu's Open command (Alt-F O is its shortcut). If you prefer to use an icon, click on Open in the button bar. You'll see a special kind of box called a **dialog box** showing you a list of all the documents that are in your current directory. Double-click on the name of the one you want. If you don't see it, it may be in a different directory. Click on a directory name to see the files in that directory, or click on [..] to go up one level of directories. If you're using WordPerfect's Quick List feature (Chapter 6, "State Your Preferences," tells you how to set it up), you'll see just the documents and directories you work with most often.

Leave this box checked if you want to change the default directory every time you look at the contents of another directory. The default directory is the one whose contents are displayed when this dialog box appears.

```
┌─────────────────────────────────────────────────────────┐
│ ─                     Open File                          │
│                                                          │
│ Filename:  [ ▪ ]                                         │
│ Current Dir:  c:\wp51\docs\little                        │
│ File Info:                                               │
│ Files:                        Quick List:                │
│ ┌──────────────┐  ┌─────────────────────────┐           │
│ │ chap10    ▲  │  │ Backup Files         ▲  │           │
│ │ chap11       │  │ c:\wp51\docs\little     │           │
│ │ chap12       │  │ chap3                   │           │
│ │ chap13       │  │ Chapter 10              │           │
│ │ chap14       │  │ Chapter 14              │           │
│ │ chap15       │  │ Chapter 5               │           │
│ │ chap16       │  │ Chapter 6               │           │
│ │ chap17       │  │ Chapter 9               │           │
│ │ chap18       │  │ Documents               │           │
│ │ chap19       │  │ Graphics Files          │           │
│ │ chap2        │  │ Little Book Directory   │           │
│ │ chap3     ▼  │  │ Macros               ▼  │           │
│ └──────────────┘  └─────────────────────────┘           │
│ ⊠ Change Default Dir    ⊠ Quick List   [Edit Quick List...]│
│ [Options ▾]  [View...]          [Open]   [Cancel]        │
└─────────────────────────────────────────────────────────┘
```

To save the document with your changes, use the File menu's Save command (Shift+F3 is its shortcut), or click on the Save button in the button bar. The Save button is the fastest way to save a document under the same name, because the program doesn't ask you to confirm that you want to replace the existing version; it just goes ahead and saves it.

To save the document under a different name, don't choose Save! Use the Save As command instead, or its shortcut, F3.

Now, there are a couple of different things you can do about saving in WordPerfect. First, if you don't want to save the whole document, but just part of it, select it and then choose Save. You'll get a slightly different dialog box.

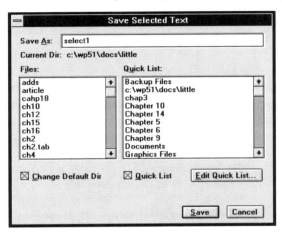

You can save that selection as a separate file by giving it a name. Or you can append it to the end of a document that already exists by giving the selection the name of the document. (Just click on a document's name in the list.) You'll be asked whether you want to overwrite the file (replace it with the material you've selected) or append the selection to it. If you choose Append, the selection will be put at the end of the document you've selected. So you can "build" larger documents from selections this way.

Don't confuse appending text or graphics to documents this way with appending to the Windows Clipboard. If you select text or graphics and choose Append on the Edit menu, your selection will be added to what's already in the Clipboard, and you can paste it into other documents or even into other programs that you're running through Windows.

To close a document, you've got several different options. You can click on the Close button, or choose Close from the Control menu icon, or press Ctrl+F4. If you use any of these methods, you'll be asked if you want to save the document if you've made changes to it but haven't saved them.

*▶ **Tip:** Appending to the Clipboard isn't the same thing as appending documents to each other.*

*▶ **Tip:** You can press Ctrl+Shift+F4 to close a document instantly without saving it.*

To start a brand-new document, choose New. You'll open a blank document window with "unmodified" at the top. Then just start typing away.

WordPerfect keeps track of the last four documents you've been working with and lists them at the bottom of the File menu. To get a document back that you've already closed, you can just choose it from that list.

WYSIWYG

As you type, you'll see on the screen pretty much what you'll get in your printed document. The only exceptions are things like footnotes and headers and footers, which you can see by choosing Print Preview from the File menu. Your font will look like the font you've chosen, italics will look like *italics,* and so forth. If you're using columns, they will show on the screen and graphics will also be in place.

Draft Mode

▶ **Tip:** *If you have a color monitor, you can pick the colors that draft mode uses. See Chapter 6, "State Your Preferences."*

Showing you exactly how everything's going to look drains your computer's speed, though, especially if there are a lot of graphics, font changes, or columns in the document. If WordPerfect seems slow, there are a couple of things you can do to speed it up. First, you can switch to draft mode, which is faster. Choose Draft Mode from the View menu (or press Ctrl+Shift+F1, its keyboard shortcut) and see if this helps speed things up. If speed (or the lack of it) is a problem, you can do most of your routine typing in draft mode and quickly switch back to WYSIWYG by pressing Ctrl+Shift+F1 again.

Exiting from WordPerfect

▶ **Tip:** *To exit WordPerfect and Windows at the same time, press Ctrl+Esc and choose Program Manager and End Task.*

Tired of this fifty-cent tour? You can exit from WordPerfect by just double-clicking on the Control menu icon in the upper-left corner. You'll be asked whether you want to save any of the documents you may have been practicing with.

We'll take a look in the rest of the chapters at more basic techniques, including the ways you can edit and format text. But for now let's take a look at one of the most valuable basic skills you can have: getting Help.

Help!

Or, sometimes everything goes wrong.

If you get lost, or confused, or just want to find out about what something does, it's much faster to use WordPerfect's Help system than to reach for this book, or any other (did I really say that?). To get **context-sensitive help** (help that senses whatever you're doing and displays a help screen about it), press F1. You'll see a screen like this one.

Tip: *You can even get help on using Help if you press F1 while a help window is open.*

If all you're doing is looking at an open document window, you'll get the **Help index,** which you can use to pick the topic you want help about. To go straight to the Help menu so that you can pick your topic without letting WordPerfect second-guess what you want help on, press Alt+H, or just choose Help from the main menu.

There are two kinds of context-sensitive help available:

- **Active** help is the kind that comes up automatically when you press F1.

- **What Is**-type help lets you get information about what an item is or what it does. If you choose this kind of help by pressing Shift+F1 instead of plain F1, the mouse pointer switches to a question mark, and you can just click on an item that you want information about, like a button or a menu choice. You can also press a key combination to find out what it does without actually doing it, like pressing Shift+F3 for information about saving.

Once you've displayed a list of Help topics, you'll see that some of them are underlined. These are called **jump topics,** and clicking on one of these takes you directly to another topic.

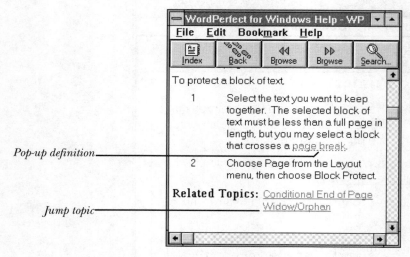

Pop-up definition

Jump topic

Other terms will have dotted lines under them. These are **pop-up definitions,** and a definition will appear (surprise!) when you click on them.

All Help windows have Back, Browse, Index, and Search buttons to help you navigate the Help system. Choose Back to go back to the previous topics that you looked at. Choose Browse to look at related topics, or select Index to get the main Help index.

Using the Index works great if you know the name of what you're looking for. But if you're not sure what WordPerfect calls something (I bet you'd never look for *form letter* under P for primary file, for example) or if for some other reason you don't know the name of what you need help on, choose Search instead of Index. You'll get a list of key words and phrases as well as a box to type your own search pattern in so that you can search for topics.

Moving through the Help System

▶ **Tip:** *You'll find that's it's much faster to use the Search feature than to scroll through the list of Help topics in the Help index.*

It's easy to get lost in the Help system, so WordPerfect lets you use bookmarks to mark your place at topics that you find yourself returning to often. When you want to mark a topic with a bookmark, choose Bookmark from the Help menu and then choose Define. Then enter a short name for your bookmark (or accept the name that the program's suggesting) and click OK.

Once you've made a bookmark, you can return to it by choosing Bookmark and then clicking on its name. WordPerfect will keep track of your bookmarks even when you turn your computer off, so you can use them over and over.

Bookmarks

Custom Help
Did you ever wish you could create custom Help of your own with personal notes about problem areas and things that you always seem to forget? Now you can. Choose Copy from the Help Edit menu to get a copy of the help topic you're looking at onto the Clipboard. You can then paste it into a document window and edit it as you like, and the original Help topic stays unchanged.

To create notes of your own, choose Annotate from the Help Edit menu. You'll see a notepad space where you can compose your notes. After you click OK, you'll see a paper clip next to the topic, and you can click on it to read your note.

✐Append

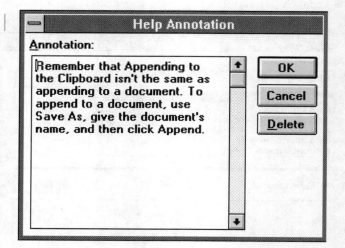

Help on Help
The Help system is pretty complex, but you can get help on using Help by pressing F1 when a Help window's open, or by choosing Using Help from the Help menu. There are a couple of other choices that you might think would give you help on Help, but they don't. The About WordPerfect option on the main Help menu displays your WordPerfect version number and registration number, and the About option in a Help window's Help menu displays information about Windows Help.

I hope this helps. Now for another program basic: menus.

Menus

4

A vital chapter for new WordPerfect users.

Making choices from menus is the basic way you give commands to WordPerfect. When you pull down a menu by clicking on its name or pressing Alt and typing the underlined letter in its name (which in my opinion is much faster), you'll see the commands that the menu presents. For instance, pressing Alt and typing **w** opens the Window menu.

If there's nothing listed to the right of the menu item's name, clicking on it or typing the underlined letter in its name starts that action. For example, clicking on Cascade or typing **c** when the Window menu's open rearranges your document windows so that they overlap slightly, or cascade.

If there's a **shortcut** key combination that you can use instead of pulling down the menu and choosing that item from it, it will be listed to the right of the item. For example, on the Edit menu, Ctrl+Ins is listed as the shortcut for Copy. You can press that key combination instead of using the menu, and in a lot of cases it's faster to use these keyboard shortcuts than to reach for the mouse.

If these's an **ellipsis** (...) next to an item, a dialog box or another window will open if you choose that item. For example, choosing Open... from the File menu presents the Open File dialog box, where you can choose the document you want to open, or open another directory to see the documents that are in it.

Menu Basics

▶ **Tip:** *You can also press Enter when a menu choice is highlighted to select it.*

▶ **Tip:** *If you don't wnat to see these keyboard shortcuts, you can turn them off by using the Preferences Environment dialog box and unchecking the Shortcut Keys box.*

Location of Files...
Backup...
Environment...
Display...
Print...
Keyboard...
Initial Codes...
Document Summary...
Date Format...
Merge...
Table of Authorities...
Equations...

If there's a right-pointing arrowhead next to an item, choosing it opens a **cascading menu.** For example, choosing anything from the Graphics menu brings up another set of menus, because all the choices on that menu have arrowheads next to them. Items on cascading menus can have ellipses next to them, so choosing one of those can lead you to another dialog box.

If an item's **dimmed,** that means it's not available to you at this time. For example, Cut, Copy, and Paste will be dimmed on the Edit menu unless you've selected some text, because you can't cut, copy, or paste anything without selecting it first.

Backing Out

If you change your mind about using a menu, press **Esc** to back up one level, or just click anywhere outside the menu to cancel all the menus that are displayed. Clicking outside the menu closes all the open menus, but you do have to reach for the mouse.

Once a menu's displayed, you can use the mnemonic keyboard shortcuts to close that menu and open another one. For example, if you're looking at the Tools menu and decide that what you want is really on the Layout menu, just press Alt+L to close Tools and open Layout. Don't bother pressing Esc or clicking somewhere else first.

Short Menus

You can choose Short Menus from the View menu if you don't want to see all the menu choices all the time, just the ones you'll probably use most frequently. Using Short Menus can speed up your work because you don't have to hunt through long lists of things that you may never want to do. So if you're just using the basic features of WordPerfect, not the more specialized stuff, you might want to display Short Menus.

Menu Shortcuts

These are the menu basics. If you're new to WordPerfect, or if you're upgrading from the DOS version, you'll really find it much easier to use the mnemonic alternatives like Alt+F O for File Open, until you get used to the way you interact with WordPerfect for Windows. But if you want to explore all the alternate keyboard shortcuts you can use with menus, there's a whole chapter (Chapter 12) that's just for you.

Dialog Boxes

In which you see many tricks for keeping your hands on the keyboard.

Dialog boxes are another feature that's basic to WordPerfect for Windows. As you've already seen, they come up whenever you choose a menu item that has an ellipsis (...) next to it. They're designed to let you provide information that the program needs or verify that you really want it to carry out a command. When you encounter a dialog box, you'll need to fill it out with whatever the program wants to know and then press Enter or click OK.

To move around from area to area in a dialog box, you can either click with the mouse or use the Tab key (Shift+Tab moves you backward). Using the Tab key is convenient if you have to type text to fill out the dialog box, because you can keep your hands on the keyboard without having to reach for the mouse. You'll see the **selection cursor** move as you move from place to place in a dialog box. It's the dotted text or highlighted rectangle that indicates where you are. Sometimes it looks just like a regular insertion point, too.

There are different kinds of dialog boxes, and they work in slightly different ways.

▶ **Tip:** *If you're using the DOS-style keyboard (see Chapter 12), be aware that dialog boxes don't let you use WordPerfect DOS keystrokes.*

List Boxes

List boxes are probably the most common kind of dialog box you'll run across. In a list box you're being asked to choose an item from a list of possible items. Usually you can choose only one. If the list is too long to fit in the box, there'll be a scroll bar that you can use to see the rest of the list. Or use this trick: type the first letter of its name to move quickly to that area of the box. For instance, if you're choosing a font and New Helvetica Narrow isn't visible, type N to go to the Ns.

When you see what you want, click on it, or press Enter when it's highlighted.

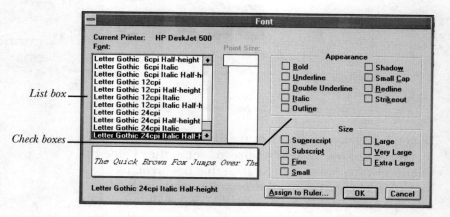

List box

Check boxes

Check Boxes

You use **check boxes** to turn a feature off (unchecked) or on (checked). Click with the mouse to check or uncheck an item, or move to the item and press the space bar

You can usually select several check boxes in a group. If a check box has been selected, not only is there an X in the box but the item's also shaded.

Text Boxes

In a **text box,** you have to type information that the program needs. Here you're being asked what you want to search for. Click in the text box; then type the information. This is one place where the insertion point is indicated by an I-beam, just as in your regular documents.

In text boxes you can use the regular editing keys, like Backspace and Del, to correct your typing. You can also select text by double-clicking on it (to select a word) or by dragging over it. And if you've selected text before you opened the dialog box, you can paste it in the text box. This is a neat trick for avoiding typing the same thing twice.

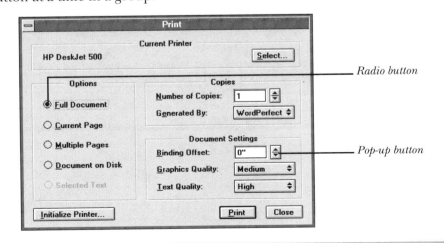

Command button

Command buttons, like OK and Cancel, are rectangular. And here's a neat shortcut for using them: if a command button has a dotted rectangle and darker border around it, you can just press Enter to select it.

Sometimes you'll see command buttons that are grayed or dimmed. As on menus, that means the choice isn't available. Also like menus, sometimes you'll see ellipses (...) in dialog boxes. Choosing that item opens (you guessed it) another dialog box.

In many dialog boxes, like the Open File and Font dialog boxes, you can just double-click on an item to select it and close the dialog box at the same time. In others, you'll need to choose the OK command button after you make your selection, though.

Command Buttons

Radio buttons (sometimes also called option buttons) are like the knobs on a radio. You can only select one radio button at a time in a group.

Radio Buttons

Radio button

Pop-up button

31

Pop-Up Lists

Another special kind of dialog box is the **pop-up list.** They appear when you choose a **pop-up button,** which are buttons that are usually marked by a triangle. Once you've displayed the list, you have to hold the mouse button down to keep it displayed.

Like radio button choices, you only get to choose one item from a pop-up list.

Sometimes you'll see downward-pointing arrowheads next to what appears to be a text box that already has text in it. If you click on the arrow, you'll see a pop-up list appear that you can make additional choices from, like this one in the Save As dialog box that lets you choose the format you want to save your document in.

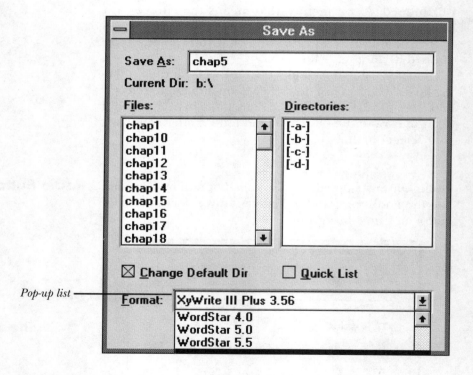

Pop-up list

Using dialog boxes can get a bit annoying if you keep having to take your hands off the keyboard and reach for the mouse. But WordPerfect has built in a bunch of "invisible" keyboard shortcuts (they're not listed on the menus) that you can use to avoid having to do the mouse stretch. Here they are:

- To open the menu, press Alt and type the underlined letter in the menu's name.

- To choose the menu item, type the underlined letter in its name.

- To move from area to area in a dialog box, press Tab, or press Shift+Tab to move backward.

- To select an underlined choice in a dialog box, press Alt and type the underlined letter in its name.

- To move directly to an item in a list, type the first letter of its name when the list box is active.

- To turn a check box off or on, use Tab to move to it; then press the space bar.

- To turn a radio button off or on, use Tab to move to it, then select the one you want with the Down arrow or Up arrow keys.

- To open a pop-up list, move to it with the Tab key; then press Alt+Down arrow or Alt+Up arrow to open it.

- To choose OK after you've made all your selections, press Enter.

So you really can keep your hands on the keyboard in dialog boxes after all.

Keeping Your Hands on the Keyboard

There are several ways to back out of a dialog box without making any choices, even if you've already filled out part or all of the box. Just press Esc, click Cancel, double-click on the Control menu icon in the upper-left corner of the dialog box, or press Alt+F4. If you try to click outside the dialog box to cancel it, you'll get beeped at and the box will just stay there on the screen.

Changing Your Mind

State Your Preferences

Customize WordPerfect! Amaze your friends.

Before you start using WordPerfect, you can change the way the program works so that it will work the way you want it to. Actually, you can do this at any time, but doing it before you begin gives you a good idea of some of the program's features that you might otherwise overlook.

For example, WordPerfect is preset to give you justified text (like the text in this book, where both the right and left margins line up evenly), no page numbers, and a timed backup every 20 minutes. I personally prefer left-justified text (also called ragged right), pages with numbers, and a backup made every five minutes because I live in an area where the power goes out a lot.

To state your preferences, go to the Preferences menu (it's on the File menu). Here's where you can have some fun with colors, too, if you have a color monitor.

In this chapter, we'll take a look at some of the basic preferences you might want to change. We'll look at other, more specialized preferences—like showing ruler guides and having tabs "snap" to an invisible grid—as we get to that feature later in the book.

▶ **Tip:** *Ctrl+Shift+F1 is a hidden shortcut for bringing up the Preferences menu. On the DOS-style keyboard, it's Shift+F.,*

▶ **Tip:** *If you're using WordPerfect 5.1 for DOS, too, why not store your documents, graphics, styles, and so forth, in the same directories as your WordPerfect for Windows directories? All these files are 100% compatible. This keeps your filing system simpler.*

Where the Files Are

Choose Location of Files to tell WordPerfect where you want your files stored. The installation program makes most of these choices for you if you choose a basic installation rather than a custom install, so you'll probably find that your graphic files are in a c:\wpwin\graphics directory;

macros, keyboards, and button bars are in a c:\wpwin\macros directory; and the Thesaurus and Speller as well as your printer files are in a directory named c:\wpc.

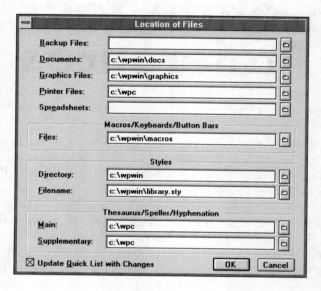

▶ **Tip:** *For more about directories and subdirectories, see Chapter 14, "The File Manager."*

You need to specify where you want your documents stored and where you want your backup files stored. Otherwise, they'll be stored in the same directory as your WordPerfect program files, c:\wpwin. You can specify a directory for your spreadsheets, too.

Make a Document Directory

It's a good idea to store documents in a separate directory—not c:\wpwin. There's too much in there already, making things hard to find. My advice is to create a directory named docs (c:\wpwin\docs) and keep your documents separate from your program files, which are already in c:\wpwin. This also makes daily backups easier, because you can just copy the documents that are in your docs directory onto a floppy disk for safekeeping. You won't have to go hunting in several different directories for the documents you've created or edited every day. (But of course filing systems are always based on personal preference...)

Backups? Not Really

An aside: the timed backups that WordPerfect makes are great if the power goes out and you can get your last ten minutes or so of work back. But they're not really backups. Backups are files that are stored on a different disk, and even better, in a different place from the room your computer is in.

Think about it. If your hard disk crashes, everything on it is at risk, even the timed backup files. For safety's sake, make backups on a floppy disk, back up to another hard disk, or use a tape backup system. Think of the timed backup files that WordPerfect makes (named WP{WP}.BK and followed by a number) as duplicate copies of your work, not true backups.

Your Directory Structure

Returning from that digression: if there's already a directory that you want to use for your documents, timed backups, and spreadsheets, you can just type its name in the box. If you're not sure where the directory is, click on the little folder icon on the right to see your directory structure. Double-click on [..] to go up one level. When you see the directory you want to use, click on it and click OK.

If you want to create a new directory, don't bother going out to the File Manager and creating one there. Just type the name of a new directory you want to create. WordPerfect will ask you if that's what you want to do, so just click OK. (WordPerfect for DOS wouldn't let you do this!)

Backups

Continuing through the Preferences menu, the next choice is Backups. You might as well set the interval you want between **timed backups** while you're here. By all means, let WordPerfect make timed backups for you. The program is preset to make one every 20 minutes, but you might want to change this interval. Click on the little arrowheads to increase or decrease the time. That way, if the lights go out, you've got a copy of what you were working on, up to the time of the last timed backup.

If you crash, you'll get a little dialog box the next time you start WordPerfect asking you what to do with this timed backup file (or files, as there'll be one for each document you were working on). If you want to get that work back, choose either Open or Rename. If you choose Open, you'll see what was in the document and you can check it to see how much of your lost work is there; you can then choose Save if you want to keep it. Choose Rename if you want to save it and get back to it later to see what's in it. If you choose Delete, it's gone, and whatever work you did up to the time of the power outage is gone, too.

Original backups and timed backups aren't the same thing (and they aren't backups either; see above). Original backups are copies of the *previous version* of your document. If you select original backups, WordPerfect will make a duplicate file with the extension .BK! using the old version of your document each time you save it. This is the version that is normally deleted, or overwritten, when you save a document. So, if you use original backups, you always have a copy of the previous version of your document saved as docname.bk! as well as your current version saved as docname. It's like having a copy of the previous generation of your document. You can retrieve it if you ever need to get that previous version back.

Environment Settings

▶ **Tip:** *If you change any of these settings, by all means keep Allow Undo checked so that you can undo what you just did if you ever need to.*

WordPerfect's Environment settings have to do with a variety of ways the program works, such as when you get beeped at or prompted for hyphenation. The program's default settings are just fine here; I wouldn't change any of them if I were you. You can explore the fine points of what they are after you get used to using WordPerfect later.

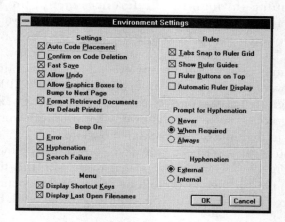

Changing your display preferences is a lot of fun, and it's another neat way to personalize your copy of WordPerfect. The Display Preferences dialog box lets you choose units of measure (inches is the default), choose whether to have one or two scroll bars (one down the side and another across the bottom of your screen), display merge codes, and so forth. Most are pretty self-explanatory, but a few of them need a little explaining.

Display Preferences

```
┌─────────────────────────────────────────────────────┐
│ ▬  │           Display Settings                       │
├─────────────────────────────────────────────────────┤
│   ┌─ Document Window ──────┐  ┌─ Hard Return Character ─┐│
│   │ ☒ Text in Windows System Colors    Display As: [ ] ││
│   │ ☐ Graphics in Black and White                      ││
│   │ ☒ Auto Redisplay in Draft Mode                     ││
│   │ ☒ Display Columns Side by Side ┌─ Units of Measure ─┐│
│   │ ☒ Display Merge Codes                              ││
│   │ ☒ Display Sculptured Dialog Boxes  Display and Entry of Numbers:││
│   │                                   [inches (")    ⬍] ││
│   ┌─ Scroll Bar ───────────┐        Status Bar Display: ││
│   │ ☒ Display Vertical Scroll Bar    [inches (")    ⬍] ││
│   │ ☐ Display Horizontal Scroll Bar                    ││
│                                                         │
│   [Draft Mode Colors...] [Reveal Codes Colors...]  [ OK ] [ Cancel ]│
└─────────────────────────────────────────────────────┘
```

Hard Return Character

Some people like to see a character on the screen wherever a hard return appears (in other words, where they've pressed Enter). The preferred character is usually a paragraph symbol (¶).

There's a little trick to getting that character in the Display As: box. Here it is: press Ctrl-W; then choose Typographic symbols from the dialog box that appears (click on the tiny arrowheads under Sets to see your choices). Then click on the paragraph symbol and choose Insert and Close. That's it. Of course, you can choose a different symbol from another character set if you like.

Draft Mode Colors

If you have a color monitor, you can choose exactly what colors to use for italics, bold, highlighted text, and so forth while you're in draft mode. In WYSIWYG (what you see is what you get) mode, fonts change as you change their attributes, so you see on the screen bold text just as it will appear in your printed document, italics italicized, and so forth. (To switch modes, choose Draft Mode from the View menu.)

▶ **Tip:** *If you have a laptop, be aware that WordPerfect provides draft mode color schemes for LCD and plasma displays, too.*

If you're working in a document that has loads of graphics and different fonts, you'll find that switching to draft mode can speed things up quite a bit. Of course you lose the WYSIWYG, but you get the consolation of color if you set draft mode colors in this dialog box. (Click on Draft Mode Colors and either choose a preset arrangement or choose Customize and create your own. This book can't do justice to a color screen, so I'll not reproduce it here. Experiment until you find a combination you like.)

You can also set colors for Reveal Codes, and these settings will be good in either draft or WYSIWYG mode. So if you have a color monitor, indulge yourself. The font that's used in the Reveal Codes window is always going to be Courier, so you might as well see it in color.

Changing WYSIWYG Colors through Windows

In WYSIWYG mode, you change text colors through Windows itself. Go to the Control Panel in the Main group and click on the Color icon. There are several predefined color schemes that you can choose from, including Patchwork (pastels and patterns), Rugby (maroon, blue, and yellow), Arizona (pale sand shades with grays and blues), and others. You can change these color schemes and mix new hues of your own, if none of these strike your fancy or if you get tired of the same old colors. Here's how to do that.

Choose one of the existing color schemes, one that's fairly close to what you want. Then click Color Palette. There'll be a sample window on the left; click on the part that you want to change, or click on the arrowheads next to the Screen Element box and scroll through a list of all the things you can change. You can change the colors of the menu bar, title bar text, window borders, scroll bars, and so forth. Be sure to keep your menu bar color and title bar color in a strong shade so that you can read the words on them. Go crazy in the scroll bars, where you don't have to read anything. Here's an opportunity to use one of those neon colors.

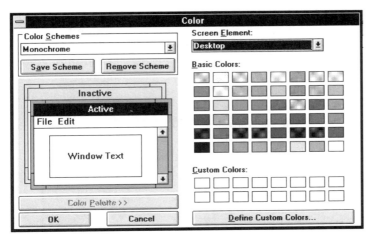

Once you've got a color scheme the way you'd like it, choose Save Scheme and give it a name so that you can choose it again (it will be lost when you turn your computer off if you don't save it.) Be sure to give it a name that's different from the ones that came with Windows so that you can use both color schemes whenever you want to. You don't have to get too creative here—Rugby 2 will do.

You can also mix your own colors by choosing Define Custom Colors and picking from the Custom Color Selector, which this book (again) can't do justice to, so I won't even try to reproduce it. Once you've created a custom color that you like, select a box in the Custom Colors palette and choose Add Color. You can then use that color in any color scheme you like.

Print Preferences

This is another area where, for the most part, WordPerfect's default settings are best left alone (see Chapter 11 for more on printing). Most of the time you'll change print quality for an individual document, not for all the documents that you'll ever print. Just be aware that printing graphics can really slow your printer down. So just leave these settings alone unless you want to specify just how relatively large Large type should be, or how small Small type should be, and so forth (the size/attribute ratios). You can also change the redlining method here. Even if you change anything, it's still a good idea to leave Fast Graphics Printing checked.

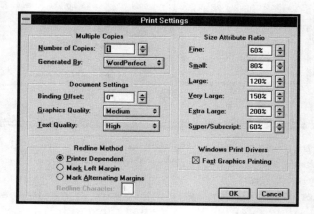

Switching Keyboards

WordPerfect comes with two predefined keyboards. They aren't really external keyboards that you connect to your computer. They're just different interpretations of what happens when you press keys. One of them is the CUA (Common User Access) keyboard, which is the one I'm assuming you're using. It's the Windows-style keyboard. The other is the old faithful WordPerfect DOS 5.1 keyboard.

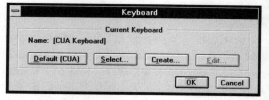

The Keyboards selection on the Preferences menu is where you can switch between them.

Once you switch to the WordPerfect DOS keyboard (it's listed as wpdos51.wwk), things work almost the way they did in WordPerfect DOS. (Pressing F1 is still Help, though.) You can press F10 to save, not Shift+F3. If you're coming from WordPerfect DOS and using the CUA keyboard for the first time, it may come as a shock to you when you press Alt-F4 to turn on block marking and get a dialog box asking if you want to save your document before exiting. If you're used to WordPerfect DOS, you may prefer to use the DOS-style keyboard instead.

However, there's a small catch if you use the WordPerfect DOS keyboard: the dialog box shortcuts stay the same as the CUA keyboard. And some key combinations won't be exactly what you'll think they ought to be, if you're a long-time WordPerfect DOS user. Chapter 12, "Shortcuts," will show you some new shortcuts.

You can also define your own keyboards; that's what the Create... button lets you do. You might want to set up a custom keyboard for typing in French or German, for example. But that's beyond the scope of this little book.

Initial Codes

Initial Codes has got to be one of the most misunderstood features in WordPerfect, whether you're using either the DOS or the Windows version. Here's what they are:

They are the settings that you want to use in every document you create. To specify an initial code, you use the command you'd normally use to create the effect. For example, if you want your base font to be 10-point Helvetica, you'd choose Font from the Font menu and then choose 10-point Helvetica. When you close the Font dialog box, the code for that font appears in the Reveal Codes part of the Initial Codes window, *below the line.*

▶ **Tip:** *You can use the ruler to insert initial codes, too.*

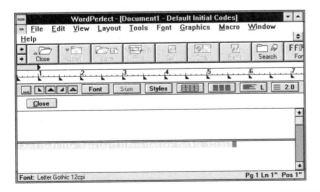

Here's where you can turn off that pesky justified text (it's called Full justified) and choose left-aligned text instead. Click on the ruler's Justification icon, or choose Justification from the Layout menu and pick Left. Why don't I like it? Because it very often causes bad word spacing in a line that's being forced to align on both the right and left sides.

Cross-stitch this one and hang it above your monitor: *Initial codes do not show up in your document's Reveal Codes window.* If you're getting strange effects in your document and you've checked Reveal Codes and you still can't figure out what's causing the problem, I bet it's your initial codes. Go back to this screen and see what they are.

By the way, changes you make in your document override these initial codes. For example, you can still switch to single spacing even though you've set double spacing in your initial codes.

Document Initial Codes

They just didn't want to make this easy! There's also a Document Initial Codes choice (choose Document from the Layout menu, or use the shortcut Ctrl+Shift+F9). That's where you can set codes for just the document you're working on. Personally, I find that it's better to set initial codes (the ones just discussed) they way you want them to be in most of your documents and then, at the beginning of any particular document, change any codes that you want to be different in that document. For example, you may want to use Full justification in a few business letters but keep Left justification on in everything else. If you switch to Full justification at the beginning of just those few letters, you can see the code and know that it's in effect.

However, WordPerfect Corporation justifies the Document Initial Codes design feature by saying that using document initial codes doesn't clutter up the top of your document and that you can edit them from anywhere within your document to change the entire document. This is true. But you still can't see them in the Reveal Codes window, and it can drive you crazy if you don't remember that initial codes are invisible except in their own special codes window. Use Document Initial Codes with care, and always remember that they are there. If you swap documents with others, don't use them at all, or you'll drive your coworkers nuts!

Document Summaries are a rather specialized way of indexing your documents so that you can organize and locate them quickly by using the WordPerfect File Manager. Here's where you set your preferences about them, such as the "subject search text." This is the word you want WordPerfect to look for as the beginning of the subject of the document when you actually use the document summary. Most document subject text, especially in the legal profession, begins with RE:, and that's what the program's preset to use.

Document Summary

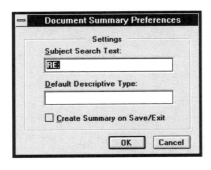

You actually create a document summary by choosing Document and then Summary from the Layout menu. That's where you can specify the author and typist of a document, keep track of the creation date, and so forth. You'll see document summaries mentioned again when we talk in Chapter 14 about WordPerfect's File Manager, where you can use them to quickly locate the document you're hunting for. But using document summaries is a pretty specialized technique, and unless you're managing a large group of documents in a legal office or work group, you probably won't need to use it at all.

Date Format

Here's where you can change the format WordPerfect uses when you insert the date (inserting the date's on the Tools menu). If you prefer a military-style date like 16 February 1993, choose it from one of the predefined styles. Or define your own special style of date and time formats by choosing a set of codes from the Date and Time Codes boxes.

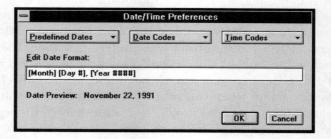

If you want the time to be inserted as well as the date, or instead of the date, set up a custom style. The style you set here will affect all your documents. You can change the style in any particular document by choosing Date from the Tools menu. That's how you actually insert the date in a document, too.

Remember, this doesn't work like a clock: the date and time don't change at all if you insert them as text, and they only change when the document is retrieved or printed if you insert them as codes. Also, if your computer's clock is wrong, your dates and times will be, too. To reset your computer's clock, use the Windows Control Panel.

Merge

This is another one you won't need to worry about unless you're taking names and addresses or other information from a database or spreadsheet and need to specify what characters are being used to separate fields and records in the original program. The predefined choices of a comma between fields and a carriage return between records is pretty standard, so you probably won't need to change this anyway.

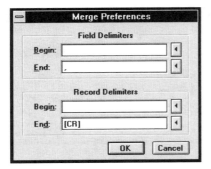

Ah, another one for the legal profession. Tables of Authorities are what the rest of the world calls citations—lists of authors and relevant papers and cases and legal decisions. This is where you set your preferences for how the citations will appear in *all* your documents. To set a style for an individual document, you choose Define from the Tools menu and then choose Table of Authorities. So unless you're doing lists of citations, you won't need to bother about this one, either.

Table of Authorities

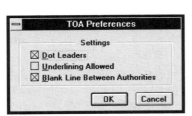

If your job calls for you to type mathematical expressions and use scientific symbols, you'll use WordPerfect's Equation feature. It's on the Graphics menu, because equations are actually created inside a graphics box. You set preferences for all the equations you create by using this dialog box, but you can override the settings you choose here for an individual document or even for a special equation.

Equations

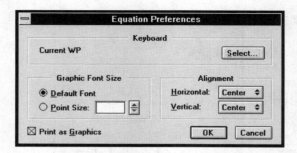

For example, you can specify a point size for equations that's different from the size of the text in your document. If your equations are very long and complex, you might want to use a font size that's a couple of points larger than your document text so that tiny subscripts and superscripts will show up clearer. You can also choose whether equations are to be centered or aligned on the right or left margins here.

Normally WordPerfect will print your equations as graphics in the font Helvetica, Times Roman, or Courier, whichever is the closest to the font you're using. This insures that you get all the symbols you ask for, because they're created as tiny graphics. But you'll find, depending on your printer's fonts, that you can get prettier results if you *don't* print them as graphics (if you uncheck the Print as Graphics box). That way, WordPerfect will use the symbols from the font you're using. It will print the symbols that it can find in that font and create the rest graphically. Try it both ways and look closely. You'll see what I mean. But don't waste time on this unless you need to do equations.

Setting up a Quick List

▶ **Tip:** *If you use lots of files in different directories, put the frequently used directories in your Quick List.*

Another thing you can do to customize WordPerfect, although it doesn't involve using the Preferences menu, is set up a Quick List. This feature is new in WordPerfect for Windows, and I urge you to make the most of it, because it can really save you time.

A Quick List is just a list of files and directories that you use frequently. You'll see it when you choose Open or Save As, when you want to select a different keyboard, play a macro, or use the File Manager, for example. Instead of typing a full path name to a file or opening a lot of different directories, you can just click on the item's name in your Quick List and open it directly.

For example, as I'm writing this book, I'm keeping chapter files in a directory over under WP51, called c:\wp51\docs\little. That's a lot of subdirectories to type or click on to get to one chapter! So I made an entry in the Quick List called Little Book Directory (yes, you can use a descriptive name, with upper- and lowercase and even spaces) so that I can get to it quickly. I also made individual entries for each chapter and for the screen dump program that I'm using.

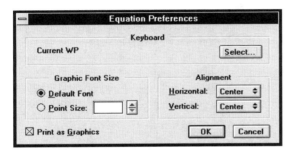

Here's how to set up your own Quick List. Open a directory dialog box (like Open or Retrieve or Save As). Then click the Quick List box to put an X in it. Choose Edit Quick List; then choose Add.

Then you can click on the tiny folder icon to see all your directories. In the dialog box you'll get, the current directory will be listed at the top. You can click on another drive to switch to it (for example, clicking on [a] switches you to drive A), or click on [..] to go up one level in the directory tree on your current drive.

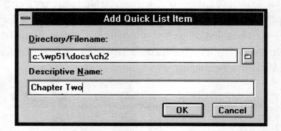

Or you can type the item's exact path name (all the directories leading to the item that you want to be able to open) in the top box. In the lower box, under Descriptive Name, type the name that you want to show up in your Quick List. It doesn't have to be the cryptic path name, although that's what the program puts there. Just delete it and type the name that you want to use. Choose OK until you get back to your document.

From then on, you can just choose Open and then double-click on the document or directory name to open it. This is really neat for keeping close track of items that aren't normally in your regular directory.

If you want to see things that aren't in your Quick List, just uncheck the box next to Quick List, and you'll get a list of all your drives. Click on any one to see what's on it.

The other great thing about the Quick List is that it has a hidden View feature. If you've used WordPerfect before, you may be familiar with the Look feature that lets you see what's in a document without actually opening it. Well, you can do that in the Quick List, too. Just highlight the document you want to look into and click View.

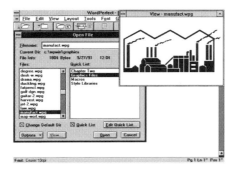

WordPerfect's Find feature is available when you're viewing, too. Just click the Options button and choose Find. So it's really easy to find the document with the word or phrase you're looking for. You can choose whether to find the files or to find word patterns within files.

Searching through Views

There are other ways to personalize your copy of WordPerfect, such as defining custom button bars for tasks you do over and over again. We'll look at that in the next chapter.

That Great Button Bar

The Fabulous Button Bar

For I have journeyed to the far land, and I have touched the elephant.

If you've head anything at all about WordPerfect for Windows, you've probably heard of the button bar. It's the row of icons, usually across the top of the screen, that you can click on to do tasks in WordPerfect, like opening and saving documents, cutting and pasting, and so forth. Instead of choosing from several levels of menus or memorizing keyboard shortcuts, you can just click with the mouse on the button representing the task you want to do.

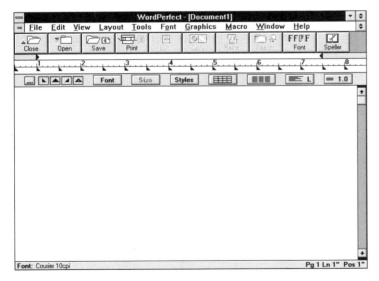

Main button bar

WordPerfect comes with several predefined button bars, and you can create your own for specialized tasks. For example, you might create a macro that types your letterhead and assign it to a button, so that you could generate the letterhead just by clicking on its button. (You can include a graphic in there, too.) Or you might create a button that starts a mail merge using the form letter you've specified.

The button bar's not normally visible when you start WordPerfect. To display it (or hide it if it's already displayed and you don't want to see it), choose Button Bar from the View menu.

The main button bar is the one you'll see unless you choose another one or create one of your own. It's called wp{wp}.wwb. On the main button bar, there are buttons for closing, opening, saving (this one's neat because it doesn't ask you to confirm that you're saving the document under the same name again), printing, copying, cutting, pasting, searching, changing fonts, and starting the Speller. What more could you ask for? Read on.

Switching Button Bars

Well, you could ask for buttons for specialized techniques like using graphics, previewing what you're printing, writing equations, and editing tables, that's what, and those tasks are all covered on the button bars that come with WordPerfect. Some of them will appear automatically when you start to do a certain kind of task, like editing a graphic image or creating an equation.

The Figure Editor Button Bar

If youdouble-click on a graphic, the Figure Editor button bar will automatically appear. In addition to the standard Close and Retrieve buttons, it has specialized buttons for rotating and sizing graphic images, creating mirror images, and so forth. We'll take a closer look at it in Chapter 17, "Graphics."

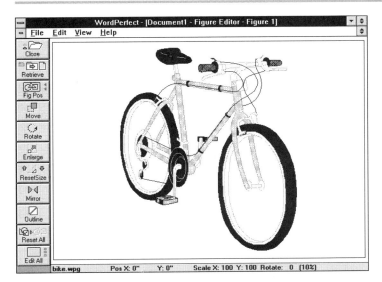

Figure Editor button bar

The Table Button Bar

If you're creating a table, you can switch to the Table button bar. (To switch button bars, choose Button Bar Setup from the View menu; then choose Select and pick the one you want.)

The Table button bar's buttons are for creating cells, columns, and rows, adding lines, joining and splitting cells, and so forth. You'll see more about it in Chapter 9, "Formatting."

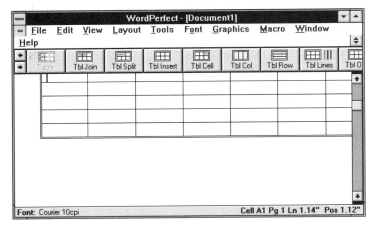

Table Editor button bar

**The Print Preview
Button Bar**

When you open the Print Preview window, a different button bar appears automatically. It lets you zoom in and out of what's on the page, see facing pages, and so forth.

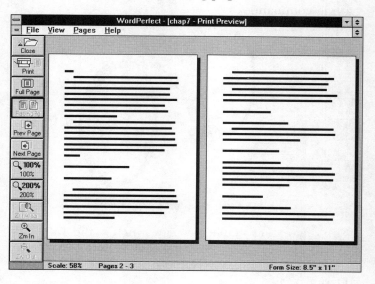

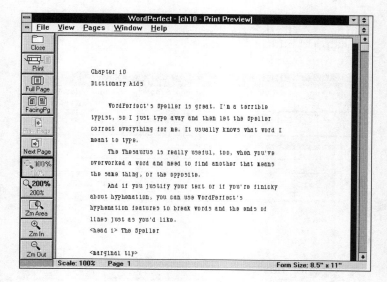

Whenever you open the Equation Editor (by choosing Equation from the Graphics menu), an Equation button bar appears. It lets you insert specialized symbols and formatting commands to "build" equations that you can see on the screen.

The Equation Editor Button Bar

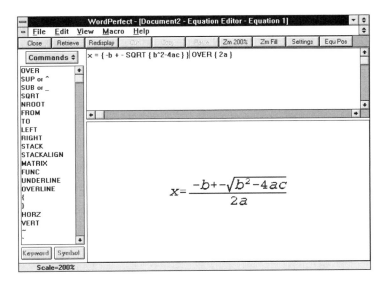

You can add buttons to any of the existing button bars, or create your own from scratch.

To add a button, choose Button Bar Setup from the View menu; then choose Edit. You'll see an Edit Button Bar dialog box.

Creating Your Own Button Bars

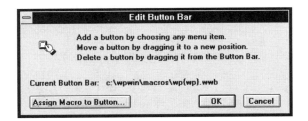

This dialog box lets you do what it says: add a button by choosing a menu item, move one by dragging it to a new location, or delete one by dragging it away from the button bar.

Here's another neat thing you can do: click anywhere in your document, outside this dialog box, Now you can press any key combination to create a button for that operation. For example, you can press Alt+F3 to create a Reveal Codes button. This is a good one to have, too.

To make a copy of a basic button bar and give it a new name so that you can customize it, choose Button Bar Setup and then choose Save As. This is a handy way for creating your own button bars without doing everything from scratch, like creating buttons for Close and Open and Save and so forth. You can do this with the main button bar and a couple of the others, but not with the more specialized button bars like the Equation or Figure Editor button bars.

Assigning Macros to Buttons

You can also create buttons that run macros. A **macro** is just a set of instructions that you want WordPerfect to carry out for you. When you turn on the macro recorder, the program records everything you do and saves it as a sequence that can be played back later. That's why macro buttons look like tiny tape cassettes.

WordPerfect comes with several macros that you can assign to buttons. Two of them, envelope.wcm and labels.wcm (.wcm is the extension the program assigns to all macros), are especially useful if you need to print envelopes or labels. A third, memo.wcm, creates a memo, letter, or itinerary form. Try it and see: choose Button Bar Setup from the View menu and then choose Edit. Click on Assign Macro to Button; then choose memo.wcm and then Assign. Then click on your new button.

Creating a macro and then assigning it to a button is the way to get WordPerfect to do formatting or carry out a series of commands when you click on a button. A lot of people are intimidated by macros, but you shouldn't be. They're really very easy to create and use. If you make a mistake, you just correct it. The macro records the correction, so everything comes out OK in the end and you never have to worry about editing macros with a special editor and all sorts of arcane commands.

Just try one now to get an idea of how easy it is. You can do a macro that automatically types your name and title.

Choose Record from the Macro menu; then type *name* in the Filename box to name your macro "name". Then just press Enter to return to your document and record the macro. (Yes, there are more boxes that you can fill out if you want to, but they're optional and you don't need to worry about them right now.)

Back in your document, press Enter to begin a new line. Type your name; then press Enter again and type your title. Choose Stop from the macro menu to turn off the macro recorder. That's it.

Now you can assign your macro to a button. Choose Button Bar Setup, Edit, Assign Macro to Button, your name macro (it will have the extension .wcm, which WordPerfect automatically adds), Assign, and OK. Your name macro button will appear at the right end of the button bar. Just click on it to automatically type your name and title.

You can use macros to do all sorts of things. A lot of folks think they're for carrying out complex sequences that are hard to remember, but the truth is that the best macros are the simplest ones. They're the ones that type text that you'd normally have to type over and over, like your name and address, or set up a format that you use every day, or change to a different font and size. Yes, you can get very, very sophisticated with WordPerfect macros, but how often do you really want to create menus for others and check for the existence of a variable?

More about macros, Chapter 19. It'll give you some ideas for easy macros that all of us can record without being programmers.

Displaying More Buttons

You can add lots of buttons to your button bars, but they won't all fit across the screen at the same time if you get too many up there. Clicking on the little arrows on the far left of the button bar will scroll you right and left so that you can see them all, though.

But if you get wild and crazy and want to be able to see more buttons all at the same time, here's what to do. Choose Button Bar Setup; then choose Options. From the dialog box that appears, choose Text Only.

Your button bar will get smaller, because WordPerfect won't display the graphic part of the icon, and you can add more buttons to it.

Text-only btuttons

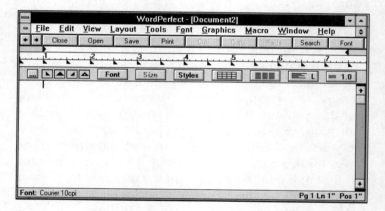

Now, if you want to see more buttons than that, choose Text Only and the choose Left. You can get twenty or so buttons on the screen this way, so if you have buttons for lots of specialized tasks and macros, all their buttons can appear at the same time.

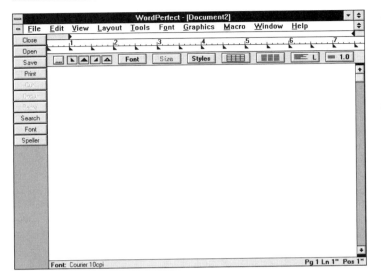

Buttons down the left side

Now for the ruler bar. Whereas the button bar lets you carry out commands and tasks, the ruler bar lets you do formatting, just with the click of a mouse.

The Ruler Bar

You're gonna love all the things you can do with the ruler bar.

The ruler bar is another one of WordPerfect for Windows' basic features that make the program a joy to use. Normally it's not displayed, but pressing Alt+Shift+F3 (or choosing Ruler from the View menu) will display it at the top of your screen if it's not already there.

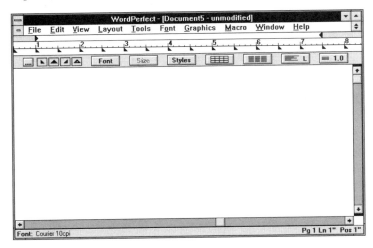

If you decide that you want the ruler to be displayed all of the time, go to the Preferences menu (it's on the File menu) and choose Environment. Then check the Automatic Ruler Display box.

▶ **Tip:** *Most of the formatting you want to do can probably be done with the ruler bar.*

There are a couple of other things yet can set for the ruler as long as you're at the Environment dialog box. Normally, the tabs you set will "snap" to the nearest sixteenth-of-an-inch location on the ruler bar, and left and right margins will appear as dotted lines in your document when you drag them. You can turn both these features off, and you can also have the ruler bar's buttons appear above the ruler bar so that you can see better where the tab and margin markers are in relation to your typed text.

You saw briefly what the ruler controls in the guided tour in Chapter 2, but here's what it does in more detail. A lot of the formatting you do in WordPerfect can be done in different ways, such as issuing commands through menus, but using the ruler gives you access to those features so much more easily that I'm going to assume that you'll just use the ruler for them.

Setting Tabs

You use the five icons at the left of the ruler bar for setting tabs. WordPerfect comes with tabs set at half-inch intervals, and you may never need to change this. But if you do, it's very simple. Just drag a tab icon on the ruler bar, and you'll see a dotted line in your document showing how the tab setting is moving. When you release the icon, the tab is set.

To remove a tab setting, just drag it off the ruler. That's it.

Kinds of Tabs

There are four different types of tabs:

Left Align:
>   Able
>   Baker
>   Charlie

Center:
>   Able
>   Baker
>   Charlie

Right Align:
>   Able
>   Baker
>   Charlie

Decimal:

> 78.99
> 200.67
> 9.95

Each type is represented by one of the little icons, and it's easy to see which is which. To set a different kind of tab, drag its little icon to the spot on the ruler line where you want it to be.

To set a tab with a dot leader, click on the dot leader icon (the one with the dots in it) and then drag one of the tab icons (they'll have become dot leader tabs) to set your tab. Dot leader tabs are often used in tables of contents and, with decimal tabs, in invoices.

A dot leader tab 100

Another one 200

Other Ways to Set Tabs

It's so easy to set tabs with the ruler that you may not care about doing it the other way. But there is another way that can come in handy. If you need to set tabs at evenly placed intervals, just *double-click on any tab icon* (or you can use the Tab Set command on the Layout Line menu). That way, you don't have to drag each little icon to its place, and WordPerfect will figure out the spacing for you. This is also the fastest way to clear tabs off the ruler line so that you can reset them from scratch (choose Clear Tabs).

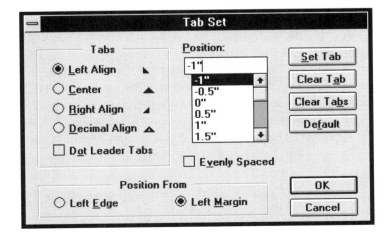

Hard Tabs When you change tabs, the settings affect your document from that point on, until you set tabs again. If you're setting a tab that you want to use just on one line, use a hard tab instead of changing the tab settings for the rest of your document. Choose Special Codes from the Layout Line menu and then choose your tab.

▶ **Tip:** *Pressing Alt+Shift+F8 will bring up the Special Codes dialog box.*

Insert Special Codes

Hard Tab Codes:
- ○ Left [HdTab]
- ○ Center [HdCntrTab]
- ○ Right [HdRgtTab]
- ○ Decimal [HdDecTab]

Hard Tab Codes with Dot Leaders:
- ○ Left [HdTab]
- ○ Center [HdCntrTab]
- ○ Right [HdRgtTab]
- ○ Decimal [HdDecTab]

Hyphenation Codes:
- ○ Hyphen [-]
- ○ Dash Character
- ○ Soft Hyphen -
- ○ Hyphenation Soft Return [HyphSRt]
- ○ Hyphenation Ignore Word [Hyph Ign Wrd]

Other Codes:
- ○ Hard Space [HdSpc]
- ○ End Centering/Alignment [End C/A]
- ○ Decimal Align Character: [ ]
- ○ Thousands Separator: [ ]

[Insert] [Cancel]

Tab Align You use this same dialog box to change the tab alignment character. Say that you want to set up a series of headings like these, where text is aligned on the colon:

From:

   To:

   RE:

The trick is to change the Decimal Align character in the Special Codes dialog box. Then, whenever you, want to use that character as the alignment character, press Alt+Shift+F7. You'll see "Align char" and the symbol you're using in the lower-left corner of the screen. Text will then align on that symbol when you type it.

You can use any of the special WordPerfect characters as tab alignment characters, too. Click Decimal Align Character; then click in the character box and press Ctrl+W.

Changing Margins WordPerfect's right and left margins are preset for one inch each. You can change them just by dragging the margin markers on the ruler.

Double-click on a margin marker to bring up the Margins dialog box if you want to set top and bottom margins, too.

▶ **Tip:** *Ctrl+F8 will bring up the Margins dialog box.*

You can keep the fonts you use most often in the Font button on the ruler so that you can quickly change fonts.

To add a font to the list on the ruler, double-click on the Font button. Then choose Assign to Ruler from the Fonts dialog box. Double-click on a font to put it on the ruler list.

Changing Fonts

To delete a font from the ruler, double-click on its name in the Fonts on Ruler list.

The Size button on the ruler lets you switch to a different font size. Double-clicking on it has the same effect as double-clicking on the Font button: it brings up the Fonts dialog box, where you can choose a different point size.

If you have a printer that will let you use scalable fonts (such as a PostScript printer or a HP LaserJet III), you can specify any point size, like 11 pt or 13.5 pt. Just enter it in the Point Size box.

Changing Sizes

Styles

You can also switch styles by using the ruler. Instead of inserting special formatting codes each time you want to create a heading or a quote, for example, you can define a style and then apply it. Whenever you want to use that style, just choose it from the ruler.

Applying Styles

WordPerfect comes with several styles that have already been defined, and you can use them from the ruler. Just click on the Styles button and choose one. There are preset styles for a bullet list, a couple of headings, a bibliography, and so forth. You can try applying these styles to get some feeling for how styles work by using them in a sample document. Open one of your documents, select a paragraph in it, and then select Bibliography from the Styles button. Notice that your paragraph has been reformatted. Open the Reveal Codes window to see the codes that have been inserted. You've just applied a style! When you feel comfortable with how to use them, you can go ahead and create styles of your own. (See Chapter 16, Styles.")

Instead of applying a style to text that's already typed, you can use styles as you're typing along. (The other way is faster, though.) First, select the style; then type the text that's supposed to be in that style. Then press the right arrow key to move past the code that turns the style off. What's actually happening is that WordPerfect is inserting a pair of codes, one to turn the style on and another to turn it off. It's easy to see this if you open the Reveal Codes window (drag up from the tiny area below the scroll bar), but it may remain a mystery if you don't look to see what's going on. So if you're going to use styles, use Reveal Codes, too.

To remove a style, open the Reveal Codes window and delete either the [Style On] or [Style Off] formatting codes.

Tables

It's really easy to create tables with the ruler. All you have to do is click on the Tables icon, the one that looks like a jail cell window. Then drag on the grid to create the structure of the table you want to have. You can have as many as 32 columns.

If you double-click on the Tables icon, you'll get a dialog box instead, where you can specify how many rows and columns you want. If you create a table this way, the program is preset to give you a table three columns wide and one row deep. Just change those numbers to whatever you want and click OK.

You'll see a table structure appear on your screen, and you can just type in each cell to create the table. You can move from cell to cell with the arrow keys, with Tab (or Shift+Tab to move backward), or click with the mouse.

▶ **Tip:** *To put a tab in a table, use Ctrl+Tab.*

When the insertion point is in a table, you'll see extra tab-like icons appear above the ruler bar. These are your column margins. To change the size of a column, just drag an icon to where you want the column margin.

Changing Columns and Rows

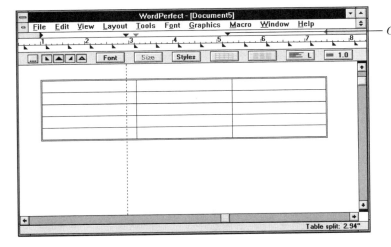

Column margin marker

If you want to insert a row, use the keyboard shortcut Alt+Ins. To delete a row, use Alt+Del.

To remove a table or a table structure that you don't want, open the Reveal Codes window, locate the [Tbl Def] code, and delete it. You'll get a dialog box asking you whether you want to delete the whole thing, just the structure, or just the text.

Deleting a Table

Getting Fancy

Once you've created a basic table with the ruler, you can pretty it up by using the Options and Lines dialog boxes on the Layout Tables menu (Ctrl+F9 is its shortcut). You can just double-click on any column marker to bring up the Table Options dialog box. It lets you specify things like shading in cells. The Lines dialog box lets you say how you want the lines (or rules) within and around the table.

▶ **Tip:** *Double-click on a column marker above the ruler to see the Table Options dialog box.*

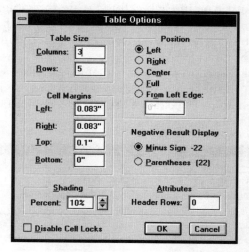

You can also switch fonts in tables just as you do in a regular document. Just select the text you want to change and double-click on the Font button.

By the way, here's a trick: To select the whole table, point to a cell border. When the insertion point becomes an arrowhead, click four times, and bang!, the whole table's selected.

Converting Text to Tables

Even if you've already typed text in columns with tabs, you can make it into a table. Select the text and choose Tables from the Layout menu; then choose Create and fill out the Convert Table dialog box.

If you import a spreadsheet from a program like Quattro Pro, Plan Perfect, Lotus 1-2-3, or Excel into a document, you'll probably want to bring it in as a table (see Chapter 18, "Linking").

Spreadsheets Are Tables, Too

The ruler makes creating text columns incredibly easy. Just click on the Columns button and pick how many columns you want. You can have as many as five if you use the quick ruler way; if you want more (up to 24), double-click on the Columns icon and fill out the Define dialog box.

Columns

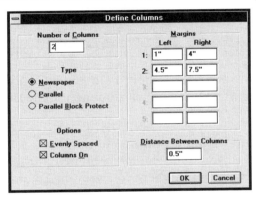

There are two kinds of columns: newspaper and parallel. In newspaper columns, text flows from the end of one column to the top of the next column. In parallel columns, text remains side by side, like text in a script or in a table. (As a matter of fact, you can use the Tables feature to create text in parallel columns, and you may find that easier; they're a little trickier than newspaper columns).

Newspaper and Parallel Columns

▶ **Tip:** *It's easier to use the Tables feature for parallel columns.*

Newspaper-style columns

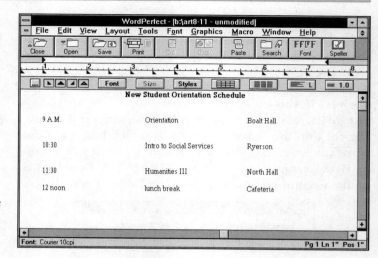

Parallel columns

You can set up newspaper columns by just using the ruler, but if you want parallel columns, use the Define Columns dialog box.

Putting Text in Columns

▶ **Tip:** *It's usually easier to type your text first and then change it into newspaper columns.*

Once you've defined how many columns you want and what kind (if you want parallel columns),just start typing text. When you get to where you want the column to end, press Ctrl+Enter.

To turn off columns and go back to typing regular text, choose Columns Off from the Layout Columns menu (Alt+Shift+F9 is its keyboard shortcut).

Once you've defined columns, you can go back to typing text in that same style of columns by choosing Columns On from the Layout Columns menu

To change column widths, just drag the margin markers above the ruler.

To convert text that you've already typed into columns, move to where you want the first column to appear and define the columns. Then go to the end of the text that you want to be in columns and turn columns off.

Removing Columns

If you decide later that you don't want text in columns, open the Reveal Codes window, find the [Col Def] code, and delete it.

Justification

The ruler also lets you change justification in your text. It's really neat, because when you choose a different justification, the entire paragraph that the cursor is in changes.

Normally WordPerfect is set for Full justification, like the text in this book. You can change the basic way that text is justified in your documents by using the Preference menu's Initial Codes command (see Chapter 6, "State Your Preferences," for an explanation of initial codes).

With Left justification, the left margin is even and the right margin is ragged, or uneven. This setting usually gives you better spacing between words, unless you use hyphenation with Full justification to let the program break words at the ends of lines.

Right justification is often used for address blocks in letters. It's like Flush Right, but it lets you right-align all the text you type until you turn it off again. You can't center text, use the Flush Right command, or use Tab Align when Right justification is on.

With Center justification, all the text you type will be centered between the right and left margins until you choose a different kind of justification. When Center justification's on, you can't use the Center, Flush Right, or Tab Align commands.

▶ **Tip:** *To change justification for just one line or for just a few lines that you've already typed, use the Flush Right (Alt+F7) and Center (Shift+F7) commands on the Layout Line menu. If you're upgrading, you remember these as Alt+F6 and Shift+F6.*

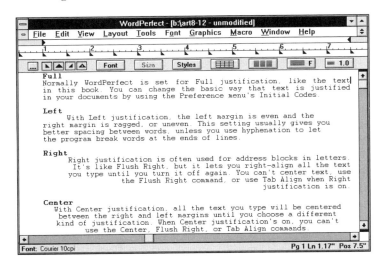

Changing justification in your text doesn't change it in your tables. To specify justification for text in table cells, use the Format Cell and Format Column dialog boxes (choose Tables; then Cell or Column from the Layout menu when the insertion point's in a table).

Typesetting   By the way, if you're reading about justification, you may also be interested in WordPerfect's typesetting features, such as kerning (to change spacing between letters), line height adjustment, word spacing, letterspacing, and so forth. There's a Typesetting command on the Layout menu that lets you fine-tune the program's settings. See Chapter 9, "Formatting Techniques," for more about these features.

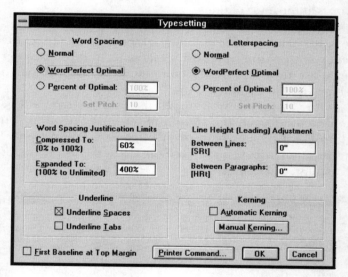

Line Spacing   Normally WordPerfect single-spaces the text you type. To change to a different line spacing, click on the Line Spacing icon to bring up a pop-up list that lets you change to space-and-a-half or double spacing. Double-click on the icon to bring up the Line Spacing dialog box, where you can choose a different spacing, in half-line increments.

If you select text before you change line spacing, only the lines in the selection will change. If you don't select text first, all the text you type until you change line spacing again will be affected.

Auto Code Placing

With all of these formatting features—tabs, columns, justification, left and right margins, and line spacing, *but not fonts*—WordPerfect uses a feature called Auto Code Placing to put the code at the beginning of the paragraph you're on. That code then controls all the text you type until you do whatever you need to turn that feature off again (change tabs, turn off columns, or choose another kind of justification, for example). So the formatting changes you make will affect the whole paragraph that you're in as well as any text you type next.

If you don't want the program to work that way but instead want it to work like WordPerfect DOS, where the code takes effect only at the point where you use it instead of at the beginning of the paragraph, change the Auto Code Placement setting in the Preferences Environment dialog box.

Now that you've seen what the ruler can do, let's look at all sorts of other kinds of formatting.

Formatting Techniques

9

This chapter has everything but the kitchen sink.

This chapter is your basic reference to all the formatting tricks you'll need to do from day to day. Instead of tutorial examples, these are just quick how-tos that you can look up according to what you want to do, not according to the program's menu system. Want to create a header? Look for "Header," not Layout Page menu.

There's a chart at the end of the chapter showing you the keyboard shortcuts, because lots of these techniques are things you may often want to do without the mouse.

Changing Fonts

The easiest and fastest way to switch fonts in a document is to click on the Font button in the ruler bar. You'll see all the fonts you've assigned to the ruler bar. You can double-click on the Font button to bring up the Font dialog box, which lists *all* your installed fonts. Pressing F9 (or Ctrl+F8 on the DOS-style keyboard) will bring up the Font dialog box, too.

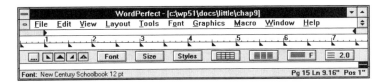

Just click on a font's name to switch to it. When you get back to your document, the change will take place at the insertion point in your document, not at the beginning of the paragraph, like some format changes (such as tabs) do.

Adding Fonts to the Ruler

If there are fonts that you use often, add them to your ruler list so that you can switch back and forth among them quickly without using the Fonts dialog box. Open the Fonts dialog box, click Assign to Ruler, pick your font, and click Add. Keep on going until you've got your favorite fonts in the ruler list.

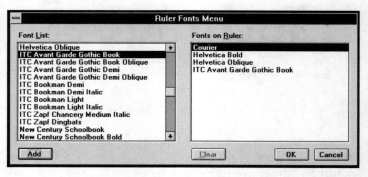

Sizes

▶ **Tip:** *Shortcut: Ctrl+S*

▶ **Tip:** *Using the Size check boxes is how you get subscripts and superscripts in documents.*

To change the size of a font that's already listed in your ruler font list, just click the Size button or press Ctrl+S, which is the keyboard shortcut for Size. If your printer can handle scalable fonts and you want to switch to an odd size, like 8.5 pt, use the Fonts dialog box and type the special point size in the Point Size box.

You can also change font sizes in the Fonts dialog box by using the Size check boxes on the right. Instead of specifying a specific point size, you can choose Large, Small, and so forth, and your printer will adjust the size correspondingly, if it can.

Attributes

If you want to change to boldface, italics, or underlining, or switch back to regular text, the fastest way is to use the keyboard shortcuts Ctrl+B, Ctrl+I, Ctrl+U, or Ctrl+N (for Normal). They're listed on the Font menu, too.

You can also switch to these attributes and choose several others (like Small Caps, Double Underline, and so forth) by using the Font dialog box.

It's usually faster to type text and then select it and apply these changes to it instead of switching to bold, italics, whatever, as you type along.

Font changes in headers and footers affect just the header or footer; they don't affect your document. So you don't have to worry about switching back to a different font for your text; whatever you were using for text will still be in effect after you create a header or footer with a different font.

Fonts in Headers and Footers

An aside, for those of you who care: There are actually three different ways to change fonts:

Many Ways to Change Fonts

- Changing the Printer Initial font changes the basic font in all the documents you create. (To do this, choose Select Printer from the File menu; then click Setup and Initial Font.)

- Changing the Document Initial Font changes the basic font just in the current document. (To do this, select Document from the Layout menu; then choose Initial Font.)

- Changing the font through the Font button or Font dialog box can change it for the whole document, if you change it at the beginning of the document. But this method's most often used to let you switch between different fonts within the document.

Setting tabs is a snap. You just use the ruler bar. If it's not visible, press Alt+Shift+F3 or choose Ruler from the View menu. Look back in Chapter 8, "The Ruler Bar," for the kinds of tabs you can set and examples of them, so that we can keep this little book short without repeating all that here.

Tabs

Pressing Ctrl+F7 gives you a hanging indent (you can use the Layout Paragraph menu, too). Hanging indents look like this:

Hanging Indents

This is a sample hanging indent. As you can see, text that wraps to the next line is indented from the first line.

On the DOS-style keyboard, press F4 and then press Shift+Tab to get a hanging indent.

Double Indents

Double indents indent the text equally from both the right and left margins. (In WordPerfect DOS, these are called Left/Right indents.)

Pressing Ctrl+Shift+F7 will give you a double indent, or you can choose it from the Layout Paragraph menu.

You can put the insertion point at the beginning of a paragraph that you've already typed and double-indent it, or you can double-indent as you type. When you press Enter, the next text you type will be back at the left margin.

Inserting Special Characters

▶ **Tip:** *Upgraders, Ctrl+W replaces Ctrl+2 as you remember it.*

WordPerfect has enormous amounts of built-in special characters. To see them, press Ctrl+W, which is the keyboard shortcut for WordPerfect Characters. Go through the Set pop-up list and pick the character set you want; then click Insert and Close to insert it in your document and close the dialog box. If you're going to insert any more special characters, click Insert so that the dialog box will stay open.

You can insert a bunch of special characters in a document and then cut and paste them wherever you want, including into other Windows programs.

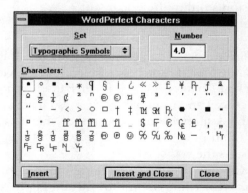

Don't confuse WordPerfect characters with special codes. Special codes are those you use for changing the decimal tab alignment character, for inserting hard hyphens so that two hyphenated words will be treated as one word, and setting hard tabs (those that affect one line only). To see the Special Codes dialog box, press Alt+Shift+F8, or choose it from the Layout Line menu.

Bullet Lists

There's a built-in bullet list style that you can use by clicking on the Styles button. It creates lists like these:

- If this is the kind of list you want, read no further.
- But if you want a different kind of bullet list, you can set up your own.

To turn off generating bullets each time you press Enter, just press the Right arrow key to move over the [Style Off] code (use Reveal Codes to see what's happening, if you're interested.

You can also select text that you've already typed and want to use as each item in the bullet list and then choose Bullet List from the Styles button. This is probably faster than typing bullet lists as you go.

Here's how to set a bullet list format of your own. Say that you want a square bullet instead of the round one. Press F7 for an indent. Then press Ctrl+W for the Special Characters dialog box. Choose Typographic Symbols; then click the square bullet. Click Insert and Close. Then press F7 again.

- ■ And you get a square bullet instead of a round one.

Take this good advice: record yourself a macro for your bullet list format so that you don't have to go through all these steps again. You can make the macro into a button that's even easier to use, too.

Inserting the Date

You can have WordPerfect insert today's date by choosing Date from the Tools menu. Pressing Ctrl+F5 will insert the date as text, or Ctrl+Shift+F5 will insert today's date plus a code for the date that will change to the current date each time you open or print the document. So if you want a date that stays the same, choose Date Text. If you want the date to be updated, choose Date Code.

You can also change the date format here, too. To change the date format for all your dates, use the Preferences menu.

Changing Capitalization

WordPerfect has a neat built-in feature that lets you change uppercase to lowercase and vice versa. Just select the text and choose Convert Case from the Edit menu.

The program will always keep "I" by itself as a capital letter. If you include the end punctuation from the preceding selection, it will also keep the first letter in the next sentence capitalized.

This is a neat feature to know about if you've pressed the Caps Lock key by mistake and have typed several lines IN ALL CAPS.

Changing Justification (Alignment)

▶ **Tip:** *To change justification for all the documents you create, use the Preferences menu's Initial Codes feature.*

There are two ways to change justification in a document. If you're changing it for a big section of text, go to the beginning of where you want to change it and then click the justification icon ·on the ruler. You can then pick Right, Center, Left, or Full (which is the default), and all the text to the end of your document will change, *including the paragraph you're currently in* (if Auto Code Placement is on). This is one of the cases where a format change affects the whole paragraph, no matter where the insertion point is.

If you're just changing the alignment of a line or two of text and you want to change back to regular alignment immediately after that text, use the Center and Flush Right commands instead. They're on the Layout Line menu. Or use the shortcuts Shift+F7 for Center and Alt+F7 for Flush Right. (DOS-style keyboard: Shift+F6 is Center and Alt+F6 is Flush Right.)

You can also select paragraphs and change their alignment by using the ruler bar's alignment icon.

Dot Leaders, Too

Here are a couple of shortcuts for making text flush right with dot leaders, like the entries you often see in tables of contents:

Chapter 233

Chapter 356

Chapter 478

Just press Alt+F7 twice. (That's Alt+F6 on the DOS-style keyboard, folks.)

You can do the same thing for centered text with dot leaders (Shift+F7 twice or DOS: Shift+F6 twice), but when would you want centered text with dot leaders? Beats me.

WordPerfect lets you use different kinds of hyphens:

Hyphens

- Regular hyphens, which you type by pressing the - key (the minus sign).

- These are hyphens that you use in words like sister-in-law.

- Hard hyphens, which WordPerfect also calls dashes. These are hyphens that won't be broken between lines. If you want to make sure that a hyphenated word is never broken at the end of a line (so that sister-in-law always stays together as one word, for example), use hard hyphens. To get a hard hyphen, press Ctrl before you type the hyphen. (On the DOS-style keyboard, press Home instead.)

There are also soft hyphens, which are the kind that WordPerfect puts in automatically when hyphenation is on, and normally you never have to use them.

All Sorts of Dashes

There are hyphens and then there are hyphens. Strictly speaking, a hyphen is a little thing that separates two words like double-click. There are also dashes, which is what WordPerfect calls hard hyphens, too (Ctrl+hyphen). Dashes look exactly like hyphens, but they make sure that the words that the join are treated all as one word.

Then there are en dashes, which are just a little longer than hyphens (excuse me, dashes) and are used to separate things like page ranges (pages 22–25) and dates (1945–50). To put one of these in, press Ctrl+W and choose it from the Typographic Symbols set.

And then there are em dashes, which most of the world calls "long dashes" and usually types with two hyphens. These are also in the Typographic Symbols set—they look like this.

Use em and en dashes in your documents for a nice "typeset" quality. The other way—using hyphens for everything—makes your documents look like you typed them on a typewriter instead of on a several-thousand-dollar computer.

If you use em and en dashes a lot, or any other typographic symbol, make yourself a macro for it. If you really use them a lot, make the macro into a button.

Hard Spaces

If you don't want a phrase broken, ever, use hard spaces between the words. To get a hard space, press Home and then the space bar. For example, dates like October 28, 1951 will all stay together on one line if you use hard spaces between them. You can also do this with names like John F. Kennedy, to keep them from being broken at the end of a line.

To get a hard space, press Ctrl+Space bar (on both keyboards).

Word and Letter Spacing

You can change the spacing between words and letters by using the Typesetting dialog box (it's on the Layout menu).

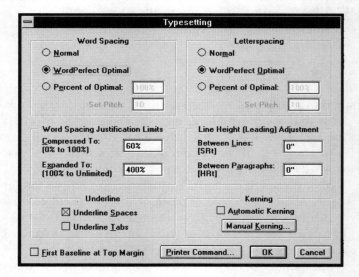

WordPerfect normally uses its own Optimal setting. To use the settings specified by the font's manufacturer, choose Normal instead. You can also fine-tune both settings, but before you go to the trouble, make sure that your printer can handle changes in word and letterspacing. Print some text; then change its word or letterspacing and print it again to see if anything changed.

Kerning is a special kind of letterspacing that lets you adjust the space between pairs of letters like Ta and Wo, where one slightly "overhangs" the other. If you use display type, especially in the larger point sizes (18 point and above), you may want to use this specialized typesetting feature. You can choose automatic or manual kerning.

Kerning

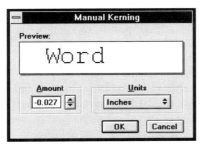

If you use manual kerning, you can see the results in the window as you change the kerning (use negative numbers for less space between letters). First, open a new document and then type the letter pair you want to kern, such as Wo in Word. Put the insertion point between the letters you want to kern, such as the W and the o in WordPerfect. Then choose Manual Kerning from the Typesetting dialog box and make your adjustments.

In addition to its other typesetting features, WordPerfect has a Line Height adjustment that you can make. You can adjust the line spacing between lines and between paragraphs, too.

Line Height

Normally the program adds two points of space between lines of text, if you're using proportionally spaced fonts. If you're using a monospaced font (like Courier), where each character takes up the same width as all the other characters, it doesn't add any extra space at all. (This extra space is called **leading,** by the way, and it's pronounced like the metal strip that it originally referred to.)

Line height and line spacing (see below) are two different things, but they depend on each other. If you use single spacing, the distance from the baseline of one line of text to the baseline of the next line of text is one line height. With double spacing, the program uses two line heights between baselines.

Line Spacing

Normally WordPerfect is set for single spacing. To change line spacing to 1.5 or 2.0 (double spacing), use the line spacing icon on the ruler bar.

To change to a different spacing like 3.5 or 0.5 (half-line spacing), double-click on the line spacing icon.

There's also a Line Spacing choice on the Layout Line menu.

Numbering Lines

If you want each line in a document numbered, or want to number lines in a section of text, use the Line Numbering feature (it's on the Layout Line menu). This is one place where what you see isn't what you get, because you won't see the line numbers on your screen. You can see them by using Print Preview, though.

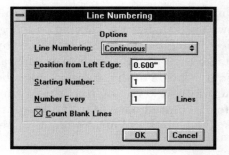

Line numbering takes effect at the beginning of the paragraph the insertion point's in if you have Auto Code Placement on (in the File Preferences Environment menu).

If you use line numbering, footnotes and endnotes will be numbered, but headers and footers won't.

You can number every other line, every five lines, and so forth. You can also specify a line number to start with if you want to use a number other than 1 or turn line numbering off and start it again later in the document, picking up with the numbering where you left off.

Breaking a Page

Normally the program breaks pages according to its settings for top or bottom margins. It's preset to one inch for each of these. You can force a page break by pressing Ctrl+Enter where you want the new page to begin.

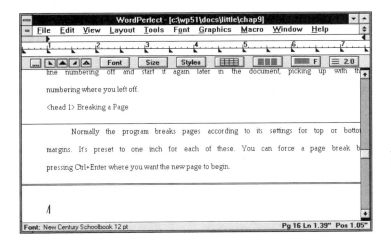

A double line indicates a hard page break

To delete a hard page break, put the insertion point just below the line that represents the page break and press Backspace or Del.

Keeping Text Together

If you don't want stray single lines of paragraphs printed at the tops or bottoms of pages (these are called **widows** and **orphans**), check the Widow/Orphan option on the Page Layout menu. This is a nice professional touch in your documents.

You can use the Block Protect feature to keep a table or chart on one page. When Block Protect's on, you can edit the text that's in the block, and as long as it stays less than one page long, it will all appear on the same page when the document's printed.

If what you want to do is keep a couple of lines together, such as when you've got a heading as the last line of a page and you want to make sure that at least one line of text stays with it, use Conditional End of Page. It's on the Layout Page menu, too.

Alt+F9 is the shortcut for getting to the Layout Page menu for all of these.

Numbering Pages

WordPerfect is preset *not* to number pages, which can drive you crazy. If you want your pages to be numbered, you have to use the Page Numbering feature. Choose Page from the Layout menu; then choose Numbering.

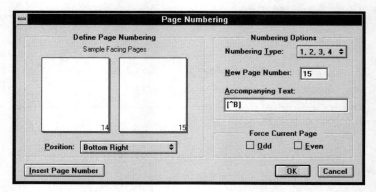

Then select the page number position from the Position pop-up list. You can also select a different page number Type (instead of Arabic, you can choose Roman) and specify a different starting page number.

If you want text along with page numbers, like "Chapter 4, page 5" or "Page 4-5," type it as you want it in the Accompanying Text box. Press Ctrl+B to get the ^B that represents the page number itself. For example, if you wanted the "Page 4-5" style, you'd type *Page 4-^B*.

It can get tedious to remember to turn on page numbering in each and every document you create, so if you normally want page numbering to be on, use the Preferences menu's Initial Codes feature to insert the codes for the kind of page numbering you want (see Chapter 6, "State Your Preferences," for how to set initial codes).

No Page Numbering

You can turn page numbering off from the current point in your document to the end by choosing No Page Numbering from the Position pop-up list.

To suppress page numbering just for the current page, choose Suppress from the Layout Page menu. You might want to do this in a business letter, for example, where you don't want numbering on the first page but do want to have it on the second page and all the pages after that.

If you turn on page numbering and use headers and footers, they can overlap. To avoid this, put an extra blank line at the top of a header or at the bottom of a footer. But it's neater to include the page number *in* the header or footer (see "Headers and Footers" later).

Page Numbering with Headers and Footers

You can make sure that a page is given either an even or an odd page number by checking the Force Odd or Even box in the Page Numbering dialog box. In a bound document, right-hand pages are odd numbered, and left-hand pages are even numbered.

Forcing odd and even pages is one of the last things you should do as final preparation for a document, because editing changes that you make can also change page breaks.

Forcing Odd and Even Pages

Headers are text that's printed at the tops of pages, and **footers** are text that appears at bottoms of pages. They're useful for identifying your documents, showing which section or chapter you're in, and so forth. WordPerfect lets you use two headers and two footers, too. So you can have one set of headers and footers on odd-numbered pages and another on even-numbered pages. But most folks will use only one, and it will be either a header or a footer.

To create a header or a footer, choose Page from the Layout menu; then choose Headers or Footers. (Alt+F9 will get you the Page menu in a hurry.)

You actually create the header or footer in a special window:

Headers and Footers

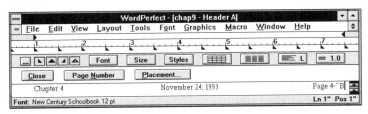

What's not immediately obvious is that you can use formatting changes within the header or footer. For example, you can change fonts, switch to a smaller type size, center part of the text, make another part of it flush right, insert the page number or the date, and so forth. Here's how you'd create a header or footer like this one quickly, using keyboard shortcuts:

Chapter 4   February 16, 1993   Page 4-48

Open a header or footer window. Type *Chapter 4*; then press Shift+F7 (Center); then press Ctrl+F5 (Date Text); then press Alt+F7 (Flush Right); then type *Page 4-* and click Page Number or press Alt+N. (Of course, you can select these formatting commands from the Layout Line menu and insert the date from the Tools menu, too.)

Clicking Placement lets you choose whether you want the header or footer on odd pages, even pages, or every page. It's preset for every page.

Pressing Esc doesn't close this window like it closes a dialog box, because it's not a dialog box. If you create a header or footer and then decide that you don't want to use it after all, click the Close button to close the window. It won't close your document, too. Then open the Reveal Codes window and delete the code for the header or footer.

Headers and footers aren't displayed in the document on the screen. Use Print Preview to see them.

Headers and footers aren't printed in the top and bottom margins. If you want more lines of text on a page, change the top or bottom margins, or both.

If you don't see your header or footer on the first page where you think it should begin to appear, open the Reveal Codes window and check to make sure that the code for it is at the top of the page. If it isn't, the header or footer won't appear until the *next* page.

To delete a header or footer, search for the code for it and delete it. (See Chapter 13, "Finding Things," if you need more information about searching.)

If you want today's date in a header or footer, just press Ctrl+F5 to insert the date as text. To have the date reflect the current date each time you open or print the document, use the shortcut Ctrl+Shift+F5. You can use the Date options on the Tools menu, too, if you forget these shortcuts.

Putting the Date in Headers and Footers

This is a very nice touch that gives a professional look to your documents. All you have to do is click Page Number in the header/footer editing window. The ^B that you see indicates where the page number will actually appear. You saw an example of this earlier in this chapter.

Putting Page Numbers in Headers and Footers

To stop a header or footer from appearing on a certain page, such as the first page of a business letter or the title page of a document, choose Suppress from the Layout Page menu.

Suppressing Headers and Footers

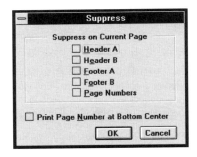

To discontinue a header or footer from appearing in the rest of the document, or until you create a new header or footer, select the one you want to discontinue (A or B) in the Header or Footer dialog box and then click Discontinue.

You use the Center command on the Layout menu to center a line or two of text. And you use the Center Justification feature on the ruler bar to center a lot of text. But to center text in the middle of a page, like on a title page or cover sheet, use the Center Page command on the Layout menu. It will affect only the page that the insertion point's in.

Centering Text on a Page

This is another case where you won't see the changes on the screen. Use Print Preview to check the results of centering a page.

Margins

The program's set up to put one-inch margins all around. If you want different margins in all of your documents, the simplest thing to do is change them in the Initial Codes part of the Preferences menu so that you only have to do it once.

Right and Left Margins

To change left and right margins, use the ruler and drag the margin markers to where you want them.

Margin marker
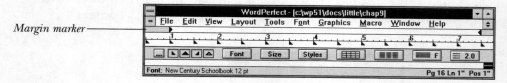

Or you can double-click on a margin in the ruler, or choose Margins from the Layout menu, to bring up the Margins dialog box.

Top and Bottom Margins

To change top and bottom margins, you'll need to use the Margins dialog box.

Top and bottom margins aren't displayed in a document window; use Print Preview to see them.

Here, as promised, are most of the formatting keyboard shortcuts for both keyboards.

**Keyboard
Shortcuts for
Formatting**

Shortcut	CUA	DOS
Indent	F7	F4
Center	Shift+F7	Shift+F6
Center, dot leader	Shift+F7 twice	Shift+F6 twice
Flush right	Alt+F7	Alt+F6
Flush right, dot leader	Alt+F7 twice	Alt+F6 twice
Hanging indent	Ctrl+F7F4	Shift+Tab
Double indent	Ctrl+Shift+F7	Shift+F4
Decimal tab	Alt+Shift+F7	Ctrl+F6
Margins dialog	Ctrl+F8	Shift+F8 M
Margin release	Shift+Tab	Shift+Tab
Ruler	Alt+Shift+F3	Shift+F11
Reveal Codes	Alt+F3	Alt+F3
Special codes	Alt+Shift+F8	Alt+Shift+F8
Layout Line	Shift+F9	Shift+F8 L
Layout Page	Alt+F9	Shift+F8 P
Layout Tables	Ctrl+F9	Shift+F8 T
Layout Document	Ctrl+Shift+F9	Shift+F8 D
Hard space	Ctrl+Space bar	Ctrl+Space bar
Hard hyphen	Ctrl+hyphen	Home+Hyphen
Hyphen	Hyphen	Hyphen
Hard page	Ctrl+Enter	Ctrl+Enter
Bold	Ctrl+B	F6 or Ctrl+B
Underline	Ctrl+U	F8 or Ctrl+U
Font dialog	F9	Ctrl+F8
Normal font	Ctrl+N	Ctrl+N

Shortcut	CUA	DOS
Italics	Ctrl+I	Ctrl+I
Size	Ctrl+S	Ctrl+S
WP characters	Ctrl+W	Ctrl+W
Justify left	Ctrl+L	Ctrl+L
Justify right	Ctrl+R	Ctrl+R
Justify center	Ctrl+J	Ctrl+J
Justify full	Ctrl+F	Ctrl+F

Wow! This chapter has covered a lot of formatting ground, but it's not the last word on formatting. Look back at Chapter 8, "The Ruler Bar," for more about using that great ruler bar for quick formatting. And if you're thinking about printing envelopes and mailing labels, look in Chapter 11, "Printing." I know it's a formatting job, but everybody thinks it should be in the printing chapter, so it's there.

WordPerfect and Windows

10

A chapter of great curiosity to all users, including those upgrading from WordPerfect DOS or coming from a Windows word processing program. And those new to Windows, too.

WordPerfect for Windows is designed to use the Windows-style user interface, which may be new to you. This chapter will give you a crash course in Windows and share a few tips for running WordPerfect under it. It will also discuss some of the basic ways that the Windows interface affected changing WordPerfect DOS to WordPerfect for Windows. So if you're already used to WordPerfect, but the DOS version of it, you should find some valuable tips here to make your transition easier. If you're an old Windows hand, you'll also see what they *didn't* change: a lot of things stay the same in Windows programs.

Running Windows and WordPerfect Automatically

To start WordPerfect and Windows at the same time, use this as your startup command at the C:\> prompt: **win wpwin.**

Put it as the last line in your AUTOEXEC.BAT file if you want WordPerfect and Windows to start automatically each time you turn your computer on.

In Windows 3.1, just put WordPerfect in your Startup group to have it start when you start Windows.

You can also edit your WIN.INI file to add the line **run=c:\wpwin\wpwin.exe.** This will make WordPerfect run each time you start Windows, too.

These tips assume that the path to WordPerfect for Windows as well as the path to Windows are in your AUTOEXEC.BAT file.

Adding Items to Your WordPerfect Group

When you install WordPerfect for Windows, a program group called WordPerfect is automatically created for you in Windows. It includes the WordPerfect program itself, the Speller and Thesaurus, and a standalone File Manager (see Chapter 14, "The File Manager") that's superior to Windows' File Manager. In fact, you can use WordPerfect's File Manager with other programs instead of Windows' File Manager.

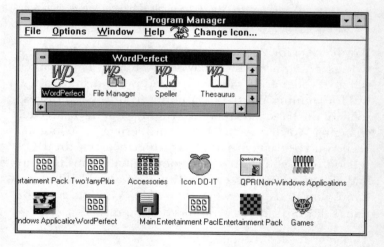

You can add items like programs, desk accessories, and documents to your WordPerfect group. What you add is up to you and depends on how you want to organize your work. For example, you might want to put a copy of your spreadsheet program in your WordPerfect group, if you work with it frequently.

You can also put copies of your WordPerfect program in other groups, if you want quick access to your word processing program from them.

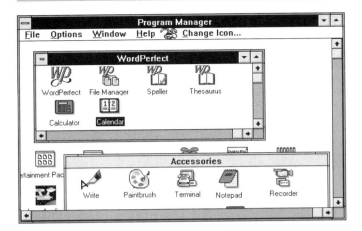

The easiest way to put a program or desk accessory like the Calendar or Calculator in a group is just to move or copy its icon from another group in Windows. To copy an icon, press Ctrl and drag it to your WordPerfect group. To move it there instead of making a copy of it, just drag it.

By the way, a copy of an icon isn't really a copy of the program it represents. It's just another way to start the program. It doesn't take up space on your hard disk like a real copy of a program would.

Deleting an Icon

If you want to delete an icon from your WordPerfect group, click on it to highlight it; then choose Delete from the Windows File menu. You'll be asked to confirm that this is really what you want to do.

Don't worry about deleting program or desk accessory icons. Deleting a program icon doesn't delete the program from your hard disk. The only way to do that is to delete the program or desk accessory through the File Manager or use the DOS DEL or ERAse commands.

Changing Your WordPerfect Group's Name

If you want to change the name of your WordPerfect group, click its icon. Then choose File and then Properties. Type a new name and click OK. That's it.

You Can Change Its Icon, Too

Games

WordPerfect comes with several other icons. To see what they are, highlight the WordPerfect icon in its group. Then choose Properties from the Program Manager's File menu. Click on Change Icon to review them and pick another one, if you like.

There are also third-party icon programs that let you choose other icons. Icon Do It from Moon Valley Software (Phoenix, AZ) is one of them (call 602-375-9502). It's really easy to use, inexpensive, and it lets you customize all your Windows icons. (Want to use the starship *Enterprise*?)

Lost? Use the Window Menu

It's easy to lose your WordPerfect program group (or any other program group, for that matter) while you're using Windows. Here's a tip that will help you. If you can't find the Windows program group or the group you're looking for, use the Windows menu (the one in Windows, not the one in WordPerfect). It will list all your program groups and you can pick the one you want. This is a lot faster than shuffling through all the windows you may have open.

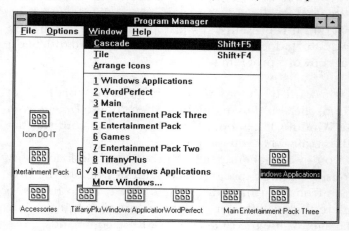

The Clipboard

Clipboard

The Clipboard is a basic Windows feature that you can take advantage of in WordPerfect for Windows. It makes cutting, copying, and pasting really easy, and this can change the way you work. You can copy and paste text and graphics into any or all of the other (up to nine) WordPerfect documents that you have open or even into other programs that you're running through Windows.

Let's clear up one potential misconception right now. You may see things like "copying to the Clipboard" or "cutting to the Clipboard." There's nothing special you have to do to put things on the Clipboard. Any time you copy or cut (but not delete, as you saw above), that item or selection goes to the Clipboard. You just paste it to get it back.

You can paste the same item over and over again; what's on the Clipboard doesn't change until you cut or copy something else. But be careful: Deleting isn't the same as cutting. What you *delete* (with the Del or Backspace key) doesn't go to the Clipboard, and you can't get it back by pasting. (Get it back with Undelete instead.)

▶ **Tip:** *Deleting and cutting aren't the same.*

And you can copy and paste between Windows programs, so you can bring in graphics, spreadsheet data, results you've calculated in the Windows Calculator, whatever you like.

You can also save yourself a lot of typing time by copying or cutting text and then pasting it again. Say that you want to search for a certain phrase in your document. Select it; copy it; then paste it in the Search dialog box. That way, you won't run the chance of making a mistake when you type it over again.

To see what's in the Clipboard, double-click on its icon. It's in the Windows Program Manager Main group. Drag it out on your desktop if you want to be able to get at it in a hurry to check what's there from time to time.

Once you cut or copy, that selection replaces what's on the Clipboard. If you want to add your selection to what's already there instead of replacing it, choose Append from the Edit menu.

Customize Your Desktop

Another Windows tip: If there are programs or desk accessories you use frequently, start them and then minimize them to keep them as icons at the edge of your Windows desktop. Here's the secret for getting a program out of a group window and onto the desktop: Double-click on its icon; then click on its Minimize button to make it into an icon. It will be there in memory, waiting for you to use.

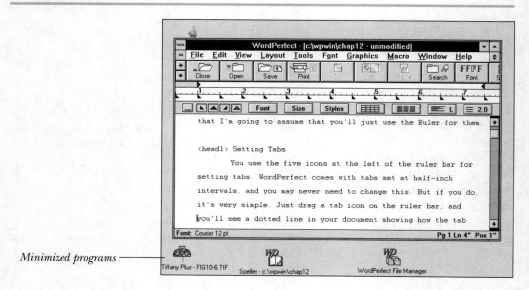

Minimized programs

Now, keep this in mind: double-clicking on the icon of a program that has been minimized isn't the same as double-clicking on its icon in a group window. If an icon's out on the desktop, it's in memory, ready to go. If you double-click on an icon in a group, you start a new copy of the program running. This eats up memory in a hurry. So minimize the program and then use that icon to switch to it.

Switching between Programs

Remember, Ctrl+Esc will display the Task List from WordPerfect, so you can quickly switch to whatever programs are in memory. Alt+Esc will cycle you among all the programs you've got running, including any that have been minimized (their icons will highlight).

The Fastest Way to Exit

The absolute fastest way to exit from WordPerfect and Windows when you're ready to quit is to exit from the whole shebang by exiting from Windows. First, make the WordPerfect program (including all the documents you've got open) into an icon to get it out of the way by clicking on the program's Minimize icon in the upper-right corner of the screen. (Be sure to click on the program's Minimize icon, not the document's. Use the one on top.) Then double-click on the Program Manager's Control menu icon (in the upper-left corner). You can also press Ctrl+Esc to switch to the Task List and choose End Task for the Program Manager. You'll get a chance to save any documents you haven't saved yet, and Windows will exit WordPerfect for you.

I may have said this elsewhere in this book, but it bears repeating. Exiting in either of these ways is much faster than slowly switching from document window to document window, saving each one, and then exiting.

For other Windows techniques, may I recommend *The Little Windows Book*, also from Peachpit Press and by "this same author," as they say.

Vocabulary

WordPerfect for Windows uses Windows-style terminology. Here's a quick comparison:

WordPerfect DOS	WordPerfect for Windows
Block text	Select text
Editing screen	Document window
Cursor	Insertion point
Exit from a document	Close a document window
List Files	File Manager
Macro Define	Macro Record
Macro Retrieve	Macro Play
Program	Application
Move	Cut, Copy, Paste
Printer functions	Typesetting
Retrieve	Open
View Document	Print Preview
Compose	WP Characters

▶ **Tip:** *The following sections are of special interest to upgraders from WordPerfect DOS.*

If you see an unfamiliar term, come back and check out this list. It may be a feature you knew about all along, if you've been using the DOS version of WordPerfect.

Disappearing Text

Another thing that may take a bit of getting used to is what happens when you select text and then press a key. In WordPerfect DOS, turning on block marking and then typing a character will extend the selection to that character. But in WordPerfect for Windows, if you type a character when text has been selected, whoops! The text is deleted. This is the way Windows programs work. You have to choose Undelete from the File menu (or press Ctrl-Z) to get it back, and if you're not watching the screen (some of us are not touch typists), you can lose the text. Be aware of this.

Undo vs. Undelete

▶ **Tip:** *See Chapter 12 for more comparisons of the WordPerfect DOS versus the WordPerfect Windows-style keyboards.*

In WordPerfect DOS, F1 works as the Cancel key. If you've deleted text, it works as the Undelete key and lets you restore the last three things you've deleted. Esc can be used to cancel some operations, but it also can be used to repeat an operation any number of times.

In Windows programs, including WordPerfect for Windows, F1 is Help and Esc backs you out of menus and dialog boxes (it doesn't repeat an operation). There are Undo and Undelete commands on the Edit menu, too, and they work a little differently.

For example, suppose you're running the Speller on a document and you want to stop. In WordPerfect for Windows, you'd press Esc to cancel (stop the Speller) instead of pressing F1 as you do in WordPerfect DOS. You'd choose Undo in WordPerfect for Windows to change the document back to the way it was before you started the Speller. However, in WordPerfect for DOS this feature isn't available. If you've saved your document before you started the Speller, you could exit without saving it and then retrieve it again to get the same effect (not changing anything), but the Undo feature just isn't there.

In WordPerfect for Windows, you can use Undo to restore the size of a graphic you've resized, change formats back to what they were before, and so forth. You can use Undelete to restore the last three things you deleted by mistake. (Undo will restore the last thing you deleted, if that's what you just did.)

Remember, though, that WordPerfect for Windows' magic Undo feature has some limitations: it only remembers the last thing you did, and that's all it can undo. Also, keep in mind that it won't undo something that didn't change the document, like scrolling or moving the insertion point. And it won't undo major things like the results of sorting text, converting columns of text to tables, or generating lists. If what you did can't be undone, the Undo choice on the Edit menu will be gray.

Alt+Backspace is the keyboard shortcut for Undo, but there's an easier one to remember: use Ctrl-Z to call up the Undo WiZard.

Alt+Shift+Backspace is the shortcut for Undelete.

For Windows Users

▶ **Tip:** *If you're used to Windows programs, here are some things that haven't changed.*

Maybe you're coming to WordPerfect for Windows from another direction. Instead of being an old hand at WordPerfect for DOS, maybe you're used to Windows Write or Microsoft Word for Windows or Ami Pro or another Windows word processing program. Rest assured that WordPerfect Corporation didn't try to reinvent the wheel (well, at least not completely). There will be a lot of keyboard shortcuts that will take some getting used to, but there are also a lot that are the ones you're used to.

Here are some of the basic keystrokes that work the same in Windows and WordPerfect:

Keystroke	Effect
Alt	Activates the menu bar
Alt+letter	Activates an option in a dialog box
Tab	Moves you through a dialog box
Alt+F4	Quits WordPerfect
Ctrl+F4	Closes the document window
Esc	Cancels
Alt+Esc	Cycles through open applications and icons
Ctrl+Esc	Displays the Task List

Keystroke	Effect
Ctrl+F6	Cycles through open documents
Home	Goes to the beginning of a line
End	Goes to the end of a line
Ctrl+Home	Goes to the beginning of the document
Ctrl+End	Goes to the end of the document
F1	Brings up Help
Shift+arrow keys	Extends a selection

More Windows Tips

Stay tuned through Chapter 12 for more about some of the basic ways WordPerfect for Windows works with windows. In the next chapter, "Printing," you'll see that you actually print through Windows' Print Manager, too.

Printing

Sooner or later, you're going to print.

The documents you create in WordPerfect probably won't be much good to you unless you can print them, as we still pretty much live in a paper world.

But before you get very far with printing in WordPerfect, though, you come up against a couple of things that you need to understand. The first is **printer drivers.** Think of a printer driver as the software version of your printer: the printer driver controls, or "drives," what the printer does. When you selected a printer while you installed WordPerfect for Windows, you picked a WordPerfect printer driver.

WordPerfect for Windows lets you choose whether you want to print with the printer drivers supplied with it, or whether you want to use the Windows printer drivers. WordPerfect's documentation calls this **WordPerfect printing** and **Windows printing,** but that's kind of misleading: either way, WordPerfect normally prints by using the Windows Print Manager.

To pick whether you use the WordPerfect printer driver or the Windows printer driver for any printer, choose Select Printer from the File menu and then select the button next to WordPerfect or Windows in the Printer Drivers box. At least *that's* straightforward.

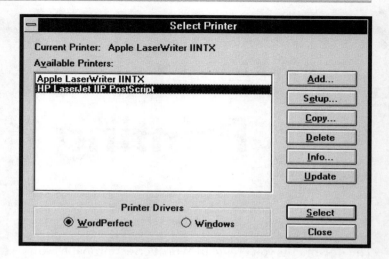

What's the difference between them? Well, there are a couple of considerations. If you pick WordPerfect and you're printing a document that you created in WordPerfect DOS, it will come out formatted exactly as it was in WordPerfect DOS. If you pick Windows, the document may be reformatted slightly. So if this is important to you, pick WordPerfect.

If you choose WordPerfect, you'll be able to also use a few features that aren't available through the Windows printer drivers, such as changing the paper size to different sizes for each page of a document. (With the Windows printer drivers, once you pick a paper size, it's used for the whole document.) And printing with the WordPerfect printer drivers is probably a little faster, too.

But if you choose Windows and select a system font (Helv, Tms Rmn, or Courier in Windows 3.0), your document will be formatted in exactly the same way no matter which printer you use. This can be a big advantage if you're connected to several printers and you want to be able to print on any one of them at any time and have your document come out in the same format (line breaks and so on). It's also handy if you have one kind of printer at home and another at work, because your documents will come out the same on either one of them.

▶ **Tip:** *WordPerfect normally formats your document for whatever printer's currently selected. If you want to be able to work on a document that's been formatted for another printer and keep the formatting just as it is, uncheck Format Retrieved Documents for Default Printer in the Environment Preferences dialog box.*

Before you start to print, make sure that the Print Manager is enabled. Go out to Windows, select the Program Manager, choose Control Panels in the Main group, and double-click on Printers. Then check the box next to Use Print Manager, if it's unchecked.

You *can* print without enabling the Print Manager, but if you do, you'll have to wait until your print job is done before you can do anything else (other than go get a cup of coffee or something like that). The Print Manager lets you keep on working in another document while it's printing (this is called *print spooling* or *background printing*).

Enabling the Print Manager

Printers

For now, let's assume that you installed your printer when you installed WordPerfect, and that it's selected, and that the Print Manager's enabled. There's more about installing new printers and adding new fonts later in the chapter, but you may never have to do that anyway.

To print a document, click the Print button, choose Print from the File menu, or use the keyboard shortcut F5 (or Shift+F5 on the DOS-style keyboard).

Choosing What to Print

▶ **Tip:** *To see what your document will look like when it's printed, choose Print Preview (Shift+F5).*

▶ **Tip:** *Press Ctrl+P to print the entire document that's on the screen. This is a quick shortcut, because you don't have to fill out any dialog boxes.*

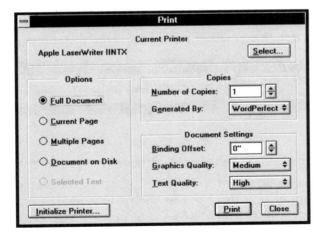

WordPerfect prints the whole document that's in the active window on your screen if you choose Full document. Choose Current page to print just the page that the insertion point is on. To print a range of pages, such as pages 5 through 10 and then pages 15 through 20, choose Multiple Pages. (This choice doesn't mean the number of copies; use the Number of Copies box for that.) For example, if you wanted to print pages 4, 7, and 24, you'd enter 4, 7, 24. To print from page 50 to the end of the document, enter 50-. To print pages 25 through 50, enter 25-50. To print from the first page through page 50, enter -50. Got it? I never have. Look back here when you want to do this.

To print a document that's *not* being displayed on your screen, choose Document on Disk and enter the document's name.

To print just the text that you've selected, choose Selected Text. This last choice will be grayed unless you've selected some text first.

Controlling Printing

▶ **Tip:** *The Print Manager is rather slow, but there are third-party programs on the market (such as PrintCache from LaserTools, 800/767-8004) that will speed it up.*

Print Manager

As you send each print job to the Print Manager, it places it in a queue, or lineup, and prints each document in the order that it gets them. You can go out to the Print Manager (pressing Ctrl+Esc and choosing it from the Task List is the fastest way), look at how the documents are stacked up in this print queue, and change the order they'll be printed in, if you're in a rush for a certain document.

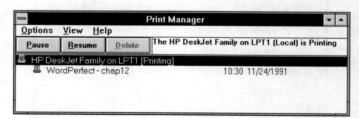

To change the printing order, just drag the icon of the document to a new spot in the print queue. You can't change the order of the document that's printing, though.

Click Pause to stop the printer temporarily (to fix a paper jam, maybe). Then click Resume to start it again after you've fixed the problem. Be sure to click Resume, or nothing will happen.

If you want to cancel printing a document that's currently being printed, click Delete. This is also the way to delete a document that you don't want to print from the print queue: highlight its name and click Delete.

Don't worry if your printer keeps on spewing out a few pages. It will print until what's in its memory is printed, and then it will stop.

Here's how to cancel printing *everything:* just exit from the Print Manager (double-click on its Control menu icon).

If the Print Manager wants your attention while he's printing, your computer will beep and you'll see the Print Manager's icon flashing at the bottom of your screen (if it's not overlaid by a window).

▶ **Tip:** *You can cancel the current print job from within WordPerfect while the Current Print Job dialog box is still on the screen.*

Selecting a Different Printer

To switch to a different printer, you'll need to select it within WordPerfect. And you'll have to have installed it first (see the end of the chapter).

To select another printer, choose Print from the File menu and then click Select (You can choose Select Printer from the File menu if you'd rather, but if you're going to print *right now*, choosing Print's faster.) Then double-click on the printer's name.

Printing Tips

Here are a few printing tips that you may find useful.

Printing Graphics

Graphics can take a long time to print. If you're just proofing the text of a document, specify Do Not Print for graphics (it's on the Graphics Quality pop-up list in the Print dialog box). Or print text and graphics separately.

Changing Print Preferences

You can use the Preferences menu to change some basic print options, such as the default text and graphics quality and the number of copies to print. For example, if 99 percent of the time you print in Draft mode and want two copies of each document, change the settings here so that you don't have to specify them every time you print.

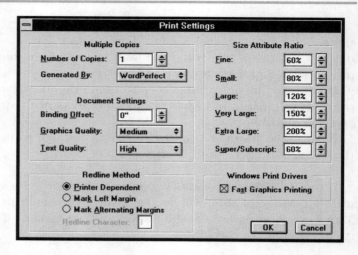

Envelopes and Mailing Labels

Printing envelopes and mailing labels is primarily a formatting job, but since everybody looks for it in the chapter on printing, here's the information you need.

Printing labels is usually a terrible chore until you get everything working right after test-printing a few sheets of labels. But WordPerfect comes with a macro for printing mailing labels in standard sizes. *Use it*. It's named labels.wcm. If you're not printing labels in standard sizes, go *get* standard-sized labels. Keep it easy on yourself.

▶ **Tip:** *WordPerfect comes with a macro for an envelope, too.*

To print envelopes, you'll need to specify a paper size and then format a page for that paper size. Open a new document. Then choose Page and Paper Size from the Layout menu. You'll see a dialog box where you can select the standard business-size envelope (9.5 by 4 inches).

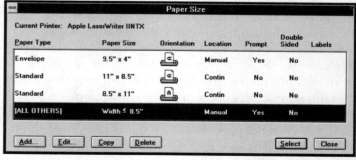

If you're using a different size of envelope, click Add. Under Paper Type, click Envelope. Then, under Paper Size, choose Legal or US Govt or A4 or one of the other predefined envelope formats from the pop-up list. If you're going to hand-feed envelopes to your printer, go to Paper Location and choose Manual. If you have an automatic envelope feeder, check Continuous or Bin, depending on what kind of feeder you have. Close the dialog box and select your new envelope paper size.

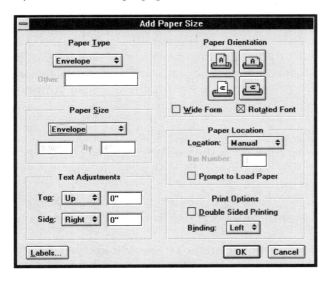

Now you've set up a paper size, but you still need to format the envelope-sized page for the addresses. Here are recommendations for the standard business envelope size. Set .300-inch top and left margins (double-click on the ruler's margin marker to get the Margins dialog box). Then double-click on a tab marker to get the Tabs dialog box, click Clear Tabs, type **4** in the Position box, and click OK. Type the return address in the upper-left corner, press Enter 6 times, press Tab, and type the first line of the address. Press Enter and Tab, type the second line, and so forth. You can check the Print Preview window (Shift+F5) to see how everything looks. You may want to adjust the tabs, depending on how long your address lines are.

Now, save this document as ENVELOPE and use it over and over, filling it out with a new address each time you need one, so that you don't have to go through all this again.

Printing Special Characters

Most printers should be able to print all those special characters that are in WordPerfect's character sets (those Ctrl+W ones). If the printer doesn't have that character available, WordPerfect tells it to create the character graphically, using one of three fonts—WP Courier, WP Helv, or WP Roman—whichever is closest to the font you're using in the document. Be warned that if you have a lot of these in a document, it can take a long time to print. You can imagine why. And if the special characters don't print at all, it's probably because your printer doesn't have enough memory.

Fonts

Tip: *If you have only a dot-matrix printer, you probably don't need this information, since you can't add new fonts anyway.*

As long as we're on the subject of special characters, there are a few (well, more than a few) things you should know about fonts.

In Windows, there are two kinds of fonts: **printer fonts** and **screen fonts.** Printer fonts are (very basically) the characters your printer prints, and screen fonts are the characters you see on the screen. Windows comes with two kinds of screen fonts: bitmapped fonts, which contain a real "character" for each letter in a typeface, and stroke (or outline) fonts, which are sets of instructions for creating each character at any size. The bitmapped fonts are Courier, Times Roman, Helvetica (Sans Serif), and Symbol. These fonts are usually built into all printers, so what you get on the screen is very close to what you get when you print with these fonts. The outline fonts have other names such as Roman, Modern, and Script. These fonts are used both to show you characters on the screen and, in the case of dot-matrix printers that don't have many built-in printer fonts, to create characters at the printer, too. They are not the most lovely fonts in the world, but they can be printed on just about any printer, including PostScript printers.

Now, if you haven't installed additional screen fonts to match your printer fonts, Windows (and WordPerfect) will use these basic screen fonts to *display* the closest match of the printer font you've selected. For example, if you actually select the printer font Palatino, the screen displays Times Roman, which is very close to Palatino but isn't quite it exactly.

To see on the screen actually what you'll get in your documents, you'll need to either install separate screen fonts for each of your printer fonts through Windows (using the Fonts Control Panel) or get a font management program such as Adobe Type Manger (call 800/833-6687 for Adobe Systems in Mountain View, CA). There are several other programs from other sources that manage fonts, too; Adobe Type Manager is just one example.

Since screen fonts take up a lot of room on your hard disk, most folks either live with the screen representation by the Windows fonts or get one of these programs. Here's a quick look at what these programs do.

> **Tip:** *Sometimes ATM's fonts appear much smaller on the screen than they actually are if you use ATM with WordPerfect for Windows. If this happens, turn off ATM and use the Windows screen fonts.*

Adobe Type Manager

What Adobe Type Manager (ATM) and its fellow programs do is install font outline files and use them to create screen fonts whenever you call for a certain font in a certain size, so what you see on the screen is very close to what you get in your printed document. In Windows 3.1 you get TrueType fonts, which will do pretty much the same thing, but only for the fonts that come with Windows.

Installing New Fonts

If you buy new fonts for your printer, you have to install them so that WordPerfect (or Windows, depending on which printer driver you've picked) knows that they're there. You install fonts in two different ways, depending on whether you're installing them for a WordPerfect printer driver or for a Windows printer driver. We'll look at installing fonts for WordPerfect printer drivers here.

> **Tip:** *If you haven't bought any additional fonts for your printer, you don't have to worry about this, so go on to another section.*

WordPerfect Fonts

To tell WordPerfect that you've got some new fonts, first select the printer that's going to use them. Then choose Setup.

Choose Cartridges/Fonts to see a list of the fonts your printer supports. Built In are the ones that are built into the printer, and Soft Fonts are those that you install. In some cases, these are just the fonts that the printer can *use*. It can't use them until you buy them and install them. Don't be fooled just because you see them listed there.

Double-click with the right mouse button to select a new font (one that you've bought) to mark a font with an *, or double-click with the left mouse button to mark a font with a +. Fonts marked with * (Present When Print Job Begins) are those that you have to download manually (these include all cartridges) by choosing Download Fonts in the Print dialog box when you turn on your printer. Fonts marked with a + (Can Be Downloaded During Job) are downloaded automatically as WordPerfect needs them for a specific printing job. If you're using a print wheel, you'll be prompted to change it.

What you can do here quite simply depends on which printer you're using and what kind of fonts (soft fonts, cartridges, or print wheels). Some printers can handle automatically downloading a large number of fonts, if they've got enough memory; others can't. If you're in doubt about what your printer's capabilities are and how much memory it has, check its manual. Or call WordPerfect's toll-free support number if you really can't figure things out here.

If you need to install another WordPerfect printer, here's how to do that. Choose Select Printer from the File menu, and you'll see the Select Printer dialog box.

Installing Another Printer

Then choose WordPerfect to indicate that you're installing a WordPerfect printer driver; choose Add and then choose Additional Printers.

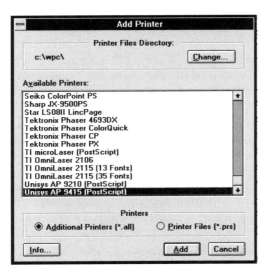

You'll see a list of all the printers WordPerfect can handle. If you don't see that list, you may need to change to a different directory, the one that has the .ALL file (see below for what this mysterious file is). If you've found the .ALL file and your printer isn't listed, call WordPerfect Corporation (800/451-5151) and see if there's a driver available for it. In the meantime, you can choose Standard Printer (but you can't print graphics with it). Another thing you can try is selecting a printer that's very close to your kind of printer and seeing what results you get with that.

Select the printer you want to add and choose Add, or double-click on the printer's name. Respond to the rest of the dialog box questions.

Then—and this is important—if you want to be able to *use*, right now, the printer you've just installed, highlight the printer's name and choose Select.

Here's a little background about what's going on. What with all the jumble about WordPerfect printer drivers and Windows printer drivers, this can get a little confusing. When you used WordPerfect's Installation program, you were asked about which printers to install. When you chose one (or two or three), the program took a special file called an .ALL file, which has all the information about all the printers, and created a specific .PRS (printer resource) file for your type of printer. That's your WordPerfect printer driver. You may see .PRS files referred to now and then, so now you know what they are.

Installing a Windows Printer

To make matters more confusing, the procedure's different for installing a Windows printer driver than installing a WordPerfect printer driver. If you're always going to use WordPerfect printer drivers, do yourself a favor and skip this section, because you'll never have to use it. But the WordPerfect documentation doesn't cover installing a Windows printer driver (they say "see the Windows manual") and you might need to know about it someday.

▶ **Tip:** *Windows prints with the active default printer. Remember that in case printing isn't working as it should.*

First, find the Windows Setup disks, because you're going to need one of them. Then double-click on the Control Panel's Printer icon. Choose Add Printer and select your printer from the list. At this point, you'll be asked for that Setup disk so that Windows can copy the information it needs.

After you choose your printer, click Configure. Here's where you tell Windows which port your printer's on. Chances are that you have a parallel printer and that it's on LPT1. (COM ports are for things like modems.)

Then click Setup and specify any of the things that you need to for your printer, such as what paper size you want it to use. The dialog box you'll see depends on the printer you have, so I won't show you one here.

See a neat little book called *The Little Windows Book* (also from Peachpit Press and by yours truly) for more details about Windows printing procedures.

CHAPTER

Keyboard Shortcuts

12

A vital chapter for WordPerfect DOS upgraders as well as new WordPerfect users.

Although it's called word processing, let's face it: what we're doing, most of the time, is typing. And sometimes it's much easier to keep your hands on the keyboard than to reach for the mouse. Especially if you're one of those who's lucky enough to be a touch typist. I type with three fingers and I still find that I often prefer keyboard shortcuts to mousing, if that's what it can be called. But other folks would rather mouse than type. So this chapter is primarily devoted to some of WordPerfect's basic shortcuts. You may have already read about some of these. And there are a lot more of them, too, but these should get you through most situations. This is a chapter that you can come back to whenever you need a shortcut, and look one up.

Mouse Shortcuts

You've probably already read earlier in the book that you can double-click on a word to select it, triple-click to select a sentence, and click four times to select a paragraph. Here are a few other things you can do with the mouse:

- You can click on the tiny area just above or below the scroll bar. When the mouse pointer becomes a double arrowhead, drag the mouse, and you've opened a Reveal Codes window.

- You can double-click in the title bar of a window to maximize it.

117

- You can click on a window's Restore icon to make it less than full-screen size or click on its Minimize icon to shrink it to an icon.

- You can double-click on an icon to open it.

- You can double-click in the Control icon of a window to close it.

- You can click on any button in the button bar to do whatever that button does.

- You can Shift-click to select large blocks of text (click and hold the Shift key down; then click at the end of the selection).

- You can scroll by dragging downward or upward with the mouse. Everything in between will be selected as you drag, so this is a way to select and scroll at the same time.

- You can scroll by clicking on the downward- or upward-pointing arrowhead in the scroll bar and holding the mouse button down.

- You can go to a relative location in a document by clicking in the scroll bar. To go to the middle of your document, you'd click in the middle of the scroll bar, for example.

- You can select menu items either by clicking with the mouse, or by pointing with the mouse and dragging to the item you want.

- You can double-click on an item in a list box to select it.

- You can click on a graphics box to select it.

- You can drag a graphics box by its border to move it.

- You can size a graphics box by clicking on one of its corners and dragging.

- You can open the editor for a graphics box by double-clicking on the box.

- You can drag tabs on the ruler bar to set them, or drag the margin markers.

- To open the Margins dialog box, double-click on a margin in the ruler.

- To use a dialog box associated with any of the ruler's icons, double-click. For example, double-clicking on Fonts opens the Fonts dialog box.

- You can drag windows by their title bars (including Speller and Search windows) to move them.

- You can exit politely from WordPerfect and Windows by clicking on the program's Minimize icon and then double-clicking on the Program Manager's Control icon.

Now let's look at keyboard shortcuts. Because choosing from menus is one of the most basic things you do in WordPerfect, other than typing text, the program provides all sorts of shortcuts for using them.

Shortcuts for Menu Commands

- There are mnemonic shortcuts for all the menu choices. Pressing Alt and the underlined letter in the menu opens then menu; then typing the underlined letter of the selection's name chooses that item. For example, pressing Alt+F for File and typing O for Open opens a new document.

- There are Windows-style shortcuts for basic tasks like cutting (Shift+Del), copying (Ctrl+Ins), and pasting (Shift+Ins) that are the same in all Windows programs.

- There are built-in menu shortcuts like Ctrl+F1 to start the Speller. Most of these are listed on the menus. You can choose whether you want to see them by using the Preferences Environment menu and checking or unchecking Menu Shortcut Keys.

- There are Ctrl key shortcuts for most basic tasks. These aren't listed on the menus, but you can press Ctrl+C for Copy, Ctrl+P for Print, Ctrl+W for WordPerfect Characters, and so on. (I'll show you these in a minute.)

The easiest shortcuts to use when you're first getting started, in my opinion, are the mnemonic shortcuts, like Alt+L to open the Layout menu. But if you've used Windows programs a while, you may prefer the Windows-style shortcuts, like Shift+Ins for Paste and Shift+Del for Cut (you can think of these as *shifting* something from one

▶ **Tip:** *There are shortcuts that aren't listed on the menus. To see them, choose Keyboard from the Preferences menu; then select a keyboard and edit it. As you pick each command, you'll see whether there's a keyboard shortcut for it.*

place to another). Once you get used to the program, you may prefer the shortcuts that are listed on the menus, like Shift+F9 to open the Layout Line menu. Or you may be an old hand at WordPerfect DOS and prefer to use the keystrokes you already know.

Dual Keyboards

WordPerfect for Windows comes with two keyboards. But don't bother looking back in the box! You won't find any new keyboards there. These are "soft" keyboards: they're controlled by the programs's software, which reassigns meanings to keys depending on which keyboard you choose. You can choose whether you want to use the Windows-style keyboard (called CUA, for Common User Access) or the WordPerfect 5.1 DOS-style keyboard. To switch to the DOS-style keyboard, choose Preferences from the File menu, choose Keyboard, and choose Select. To switch back to the Windows-style keyboard, do the same thing, but choose Default (CUA) instead of Select.

But switching keyboards back to one you thought you knew already isn't quite that simple. The DOS-style keyboard is very similar to the one WordPerfect 5.1 users were used to, but there are some subtle differences. Some of the keyboard shortcuts you were used to won't work any more, and there are a few new ones, too.

The Ctrl-Key Secret: Bypassing the Menus

But here's one secret that will help you: *There are Ctrl-key shortcuts that are the same on both keyboards.* You can use all these on both keyboards instead of memorizing new shortcuts:

Print	Ctrl+P
Undo	Ctrl+Z (think of it as the WiZard)
Go To	Ctrl+G
Cut	Ctrl+X
Copy	Ctrl+C
Paste	Ctrl+V
Justify Left	Ctrl+L
Justify Full	Ctrl+F
Justify Right	Ctrl+R

Justify Center	Ctrl+J
Normal Font	Ctrl+N
Bold	Ctrl+B
Italics	Ctrl-I
Underline	Ctrl+U
Size	Ctrl+S
WP Characters	Ctrl+W

Fine point: Some of these shortcuts can't be used if you've pulled a menu down and there's another shortcut listed for it on that menu. For example, if you're displaying the Edit menu, WordPerfect wants you to use Shift+Del to cut, not Ctrl+X. If you're not displaying a menu, all of these Ctrl key shortcuts will work. That's what they're designed to do: to speed things up by letting you bypass the menus.

Other Shortcuts

There are a lot of other keyboard shortcuts that you can use for doing things like moving through your document, deleting text, and so forth. For example, Ctrl+Home takes you to the beginning of a document, and Ctrl+End takes you to the end. Here are a few others for the standard CUA keyboard:

To move to	Press
The end of the line	End
The bottom of the page	Alt+End
A specific page	Ctrl+G
Up one screen	PgUp
Down one screen	PgDn
To the next document	Ctrl+F6
To the previous document	Ctrl+Shift+F6

There are also shortcuts for managing documents, like these:

Save   Shift+F3

Save As   F3

Clear document   Ctrl+Shift+F4

New   Shift+F4

Close document   Ctrl+F4

And shortcuts for selecting text:

Up one line   Shift+Up arrow

Down one line   Shift+Down arrow

Previous paragraph   Ctrl+Shift+Up arrow

Next paragraph   Ctrl+Shift+Down arrow

More shortcuts, for deleting text:

Delete the current word   Ctrl+Bksp

Delete to the end of the line   Ctrl+Del

Delete to the end of the page   Ctrl+Shift+Del

Believe me, these are not all the keyboard shortcuts, but they give you a good idea of the basic ones.

Make Your Own Shortcuts

In fact, you can reassign keys on your keyboard and even create new keyboards. You can assign special characters to certain key combinations, too, so that you can type mathematical or foreign-language characters quickly. You can even assign macros to keys or have the program type text automatically when you press a key.

To edit a keyboard, you use the Preferences menu, choose Keyboard, select a keyboard to edit, and choose Edit. You'll see a list of items (commands, menus, macros, text) that you can assign to keys.

This is a pretty advanced technique, so we won't go into it very deeply here, but I will tell you one secret: edit a copy of an existing keyboard instead of trying to create one from scratch. Then just save it under a different name than the original keyboard so that you don't overwrite one of your basic keyboards.

Just to give you an idea of what's involved, say that you want to assign the infinity symbol to a key combination Ctrl+Shift+I (you can use Ctrl, Alt, Shift, Alt+Shift, and Ctrl+Shift combinations). Here's how to do that.

1. In a document, press Ctrl+W to get the Character Set dialog box.

2. Choose the Math/Scientific character set. Insert the symbol and close the dialog box.

3. Highlight the symbol and copy it (Ctrl+C).

4. Choose Preferences from the Edit menu; then choose Keyboard.

5. Select the keyboard you want to edit. Choose Copy from the Options box and give the copy a new name. (Edit a copy of a keyboard so that the original stays unchanged.)

6. Select the newly named copy; then choose to edit it.

7. Next to Item Types, choose Text.

8. Type *infinity* in the Name box. Press Tab to move to the Text box. Then press Shift+Ins to paste the symbol.

9. Click on "infinity" to highlight its name. Press Ctrl+Shift+I and click Assign. Then click OK until you get back to your document.

Tips for Making the Big Switch

You can't expect to learn all of the program's shortcuts right away, even if you're not already confused by switching from WordPerfect DOS to WordPerfect for Windows. The best thing to do until you get used to the changes (or the program itself, if you're brand-new to it) is to use the mouse and read what's on the menus. Then use the mnemonic shortcuts, like Alt+M P for Macro Play.

If you plan to use other Windows programs, it's a good idea to get used to WordPerfect's Windows-style keyboard instead of depending on the WordPerfect DOS keyboard, even for a little while. Other Windows programs will use the same kinds of shortcuts as part of the standard Windows interface.

Mixing is OK   If you really want to use the function key shortcuts, re-member that they're listed on the menus. They're really the fastest of all because you don't have to pull down a menu to use them. In fact, you can use the mnemonics, the function key shortcuts, and the mouse, or a mixture of all of them.

Rely on the Button Bar   Another thing to do to help ease the transition is to use the Button Bar (see Chapter 7, "The Fabulous Button Bar," if you haven't already read it). WordPerfect for Windows comes with a predefined Button Bar with icons for Close, Open, Save, Print, Cut, Copy Paste, Search, Font, and Speller. These are all the most common tasks, so use the buttons until you get used to the new keyboard short-cuts.

Searching and Replacing

In which you discover how powerful these features really are.

Why a whole chapter on searching and replacing? Because it's one of the most powerful tools you can use in any word processing program.

To locate a specific word, phrase, or formatting code, the fastest way is probably to use the keyboard shortcut F2 or click the Search button on the button bar. (Search is also on the Edit menu.) You can search forward or backward through a document.

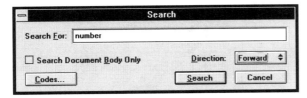

Normally WordPerfect searches only through the document text, but you can also do an extended search by unchecking the Search Document Body Only Box. Then the program will search headers and footers, footnotes, endnotes, graphics box captions, text boxes, and so forth.

To use the keyboard instead of the menus, press F2 for a forward search, Shift+F2 to search for the next occurrence of something you already searched for, or Alt+F2 to search for the previous occurrence.

Searching

▶ **Tip:** *Don't waste time scrolling through a document. Use the Search feature to go quickly to a word that's near where you want to go.*

▶ **Tip:** *Keyboard shortcut for switching directions in the Search dialog box: Tab Tab Down arrow, even if you want to search backward.*

▶ **Tip:** *These shortcuts are thankfully the same on both keyboards!*

In the Search For box, type the characters you want to search for (I'll give you some tips for that later). Use as many characters as you need to identify exactly what you're looking for. For example, don't look for *the* unless you want to find a lot of them! You can also just look for parts of words, like *encyc* for encyclopedia. If what the program finds isn't what you want, press Shift+F2 to search for the same thing again.

To start the search, press Enter. If you're used to WordPerfect DOS, you'll try to press F2 but nothing will happen. (This drives you nuts until you get used to it in WordPerfect for Windows.)

Entering Search Patterns

As long as you enter text in lowercase letters, WordPerfect will look for it as either uppercase or lowercase. For example, if you enter *brown*, it will find both brown and Brown. (It will find browned, browning, and so forth, too, so if you want to search for a whole word, put a space before and after it.) If you enter text in uppercase, it will only find the exact match: entering *Brown* finds Brown (and Browning, etc.)

Searching for Codes

You can also search for formatting codes. Choose Codes from the Search dialog box; then double-click on the code you want to search for in the Search Codes dialog box.

For example, having a variety of different tab settings in a document can often cause formatting problems. You can search for any extra tab settings and remove them.

You can search for special characters by pressing Ctrl+W when the insertion point is in the Search For box. You'll see the WordPerfect Characters dialog box. Pick your character set, highlight the character you want to search for, and click Insert and Close to insert it and get rid of the dialog box.

Searching for Special Characters

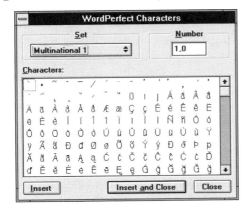

Say that you want to search for the paragraph symbol (¶). It's in the Typographic Symbols set, so click on Set, choose Typographic Symbols, and find the paragraph symbol.

If you want to search for a word or phrase and replace it with another, choose Replace from the Edit menu, or press Ctrl+F2. You'll get the Search and Replace dialog box.

Searching and Replacing

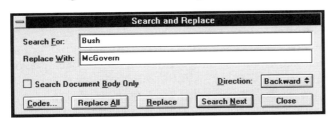

▶ **Tip:** *To save typing time, abbreviate long or complicated words as you type and then replace them with the spelled-out version. Type* Zam *and replace it with* Zamczyk, *for example.*

Then type the characters to search for and the characters that are to be the replacements. You can press Tab to move quickly from the Search For box to the Replace With box.

If you enter the search text in lowercase, the program will search for both uppercase and lowercase. Your replacement text will be replaced just exactly as you typed it, unless the program locates the search text in uppercase. Then the replacement text will be capitalized, too.

Press Enter or click Search Next to search for the first occurrence but not actually replace it. This is the safest thing to do because it lets you see exactly what the program is going to work on. (You may need to drag the dialog box out of the way to see what's going on in the document. Put it "upstairs," up near the title bar and button bar.)

Once the program has found what you're searching for, you can click back in the document to edit it. The dialog box won't go away until you click Close or double-click in its Control menu icon, so you can search, edit the document, and search again. Just click Search Next in the dialog box to search for the next occurrence. This saves you clicking once to activate the dialog box and then pressing Enter to choose Search Next.

It's easy to make mistakes with search-and-replace because the program will do *exactly* what you tell it to. For example, if you've spelled a name as Brown throughout your document and later realize that it should be spelled Braun, you might think that you could just search for *own* and replace it with *aun*. Well, that will certainly replace Brown with Braun, but it will also replace *browning* with *brauning, owning* with *auning, renowned* with *renauned,* and so on. To get the best results with search-and-replace, be as specific as you can about what you're replacing with what.

▶ **Tip:** *To strip out every occurrence of something in a document, search for it and replace it with nothing, by clicking Replace All.*

Clicking Replace All to make all the replacements at once may not be as dangerous as it seems, because you can Undo the results of a search-and-replace operation if you immediately realize that you've made a mistake and choose Undo.

If you've done something else and Undo is no longer available for undoing a replacement, there may still be a way out if you've muddled everything up but you haven't saved your document yet. Just close it without saving it and then open it again to get the last-saved version back. Hopefully this is the one you saved before you made all the replacements. This is also why it's a good idea to save your document before you do a search-and-replace.

Don't Forget the File Manager

Remember that the File Manager has some very sophisticated features that let you locate specific words in documents. If you're looking for a certain document that you know contains a word or phrase instead of looking for a particular location within a certain document, you'll find that it's faster to use the File Manager (Chapter 14) than open a bunch of documents and search through them.

The File Manager

Lord of the Files. WordPerfect for Windows does file management better than Windows!

WordPerfect's File Manager is better than Windows' File Manager. So there, Windows. It lets you do a lot more, and it's a lot easier to use. As a matter of fact, because it's a standalone program you can use it *instead* of Windows' File Manager with your other Windows programs. It doesn't require WordPerfect for Windows to run (but it does require Windows). And it lets you do things that the Windows File Manager never dreamed of. Spend five or ten minutes with it and you'll see what I mean.

The File Manager lets you

- View your directory system to see what's in directories
- See what's in files—including graphics and in color if you have a color monitor
- Look at detailed information about your files
- Change the order information is presented on the screen
- Customize its button bar (yes, the File Manager has its own menu bar and button bar)
- Search through files for specific words
- Search through directories and disks for specific files
- See what's on different drives
- Get information about your system, about Windows, about your disks

- Set up and edit a Quick List of files and directories you use most often
- Print documents
- Start other programs running
- Associate particular types of files with the programs they belong to
- Copy, delete, and move files
- Rename files and directories
- Create directories.

That's just a sampling. It actually does more than all this, and you can get used to using it very quickly.

Directories   Before you begin using the File Manager, there are a few basic ideas that you need to be familiar with about how things are stored on your computer. If you've been using a computer for a while, you can skip this section, because we're going to talk about files and directories and what they are.

On your computer, files are organized into a system of **directories.** It's easy to be able to think of a directory as a file folder in your filing cabinet. You can put all kinds of files in a directory—programs, different documents, graphics, whatever you like. Directories can even hold other directories, which are called **subdirectories,** just as you stuff folders inside other folders in a filing cabinet.

If you've got subdirectories within subdirectories within subdirectories, you can get pretty deep in the filing system. That's where the **path** comes in. The path is just a list of all the directories that lead to the directory that contains the file that you're looking for, like the house that Jack built. You saw path names when you installed WordPerfect for Windows and the installation program told you which directories files were being put in. In a path, each directory is separated with a backslash, so c:\wpwin\docs is the path to a subdirectory named docs under the wpwin directory on drive C.

Once you're in WordPerfect, you can use the Preferences menu (it's on the File menu) to specify other directories you want to store files in. (See Chapter 6, "State Your Preferences.") But to create new directories, move files from one directory to another, change file names and directory names, delete files, copy files, and so forth, you use the File Manager. It's WordPerfect for Windows' utility for letting you do your computer "housekeeping"—moving files around, viewing what's stored on a disk, locating a particular file, and so forth.

> ▶ **Tip:** *You can also copy, delete, and rename files by clicking the Options button in an Open, Save, or Save As dialog box in WordPerfect itself.*

To get to the File Manager if you've got WordPerfect running, choose it from the File menu or use the keyboard shortcut Alt+F F. You can add a button for it to your button bar if you like; see Chapter 7.

Going to the File Manager

The File Manager has five different types of windows:

- The Navigator lets you move through directories
- The Viewer shows you what's in individual files
- File Lists give you detailed information about files, such as the date and time they were last saved, how big they are, and so forth
- The Quick List is a custom list you set up of the documents and directories you use most often (you saw it back in Chapter 6, "State Your Preferences")
- A Search Results window shows you the results of some pretty sophisticated searches you can make through the File Manager.

File Manager Windows

> ▶ **Tip:** *You can start the File Manager from Windows' Program Manager without starting WordPerfect. Once you double-click on a document in the File Manager, you'll start WordPerfect running and open the document at the same time.*

The arrangement you normally see unless you choose one of the other arrangements shows you the Navigator on top and the Viewer on the bottom. As you navigate through directories, a little hand will point to the next level as you open directories to see what's inside them. Directory names are in [brackets], like this, and they're normally at the beginning of each list. When you've gone as far as you can down one branch of directories and subdirectories, you won't see the File Manager's little hand, because there'll be no more directories to open.

> ▶ **Tip:** *You can move all of the File Manager's windows separately from each other. Just drag them by their title bars.*

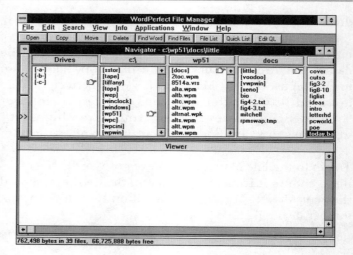

Navigator and Viewer

Seeing What's What

To change to a different directory and see what's in it, double-click on its name. To see what's in a file (in the Viewer), click on it once. If you double-click on the name of a WordPerfect document, you'll open that document. If WordPerfect hasn't been started yet, double-clicking on a WordPerfect document will start the program, too, so this is a quick way to start WordPerfect and open the first document you want to work with at the same time.

You can open more directories in the File Manager than it can display on the screen. To see in other directories, click on the Navigator's right button or press the Left arrow key.

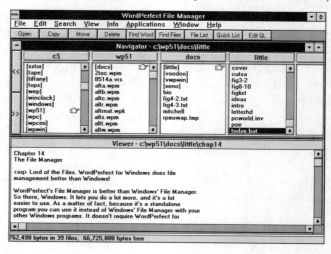

The Viewer shows you what's in files

You use the View menu and choose Layouts to pick the basic File Manager layout you want to use. There are lots of choices, and the one you pick doesn't especially matter, because you can open the different types of windows individually, too.

Choosing What to See

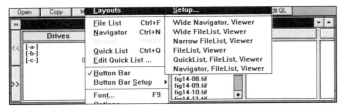

For example, you might want to see just a wide view of the Navigator and a regular window of the Viewer if you're reorganizing directories. Or choose a wide File List and a viewer if you're looking in a lot of different files.

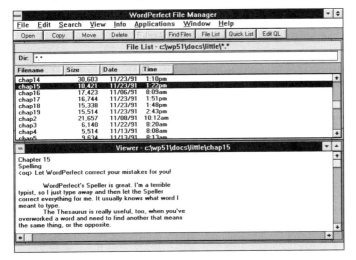

File List and Viewer

You can pick File List and Viewer to see details about your files and view what's in them, too. Choosing Quick List, File List, and Viewer lets you see your Quick List as well as the other views, and it's easy to pick new files to add to your Quick List this way.

Navigator, File List, and Viewer probably gives you the most flexible basic setup, because you can easily move through directories, see details about files, and view what's in them, all at the same time.

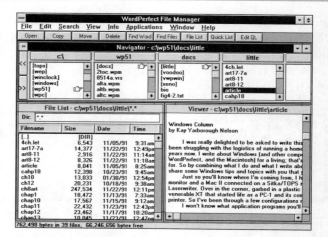

Navigator, File List, and Viewer

But say that you're looking at a File List and the Viewer and you want to see the Navigator. No problem. Just press Ctrl+N to bring it up. Want to see your Quick List? Do a Ctrl+Q. To see a File List, use Ctrl+F.

Looking at Two Different Things

You can open more than one Navigator window and more than one File List window, too. This is how you can see what's on two different drives at once or look into separate branches of your directory tree system. Say that you want to copy files from your hard disk (drive C) to a floppy disk in drive A, and you want to see what's already on the disk in drive A. Just open a Navigator window for drive C and one for drive A, too.

▶ **Tip:** *To resize a File Manager window, move the mouse pointer to a border of the window (top, side, whatever) until it becomes a double arrowhead. Then drag.*

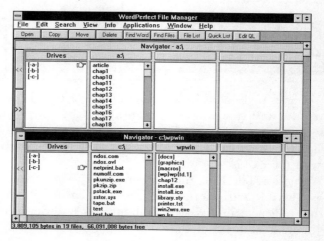

Things can get cluttered in a hurry if you open a lot of File Manager windows, so keep in mind one basic rule while you're using the File Manager: *If you can't see what you're looking for, Tile windows to see what's in them* (Shift+F4 is the keyboard shortcut for Tile).

Lost? Tile Your Windows

The File Manager's Viewer will show you what's actually in a file. If the file you click on is a program file (an executable file, like Quattro Pro or anything else that ends in .exe or .com), all you'll see in the Viewer is garbage. If the file is a WordPerfect file or a text file (one that doesn't have any formatting codes in it), you'll see exactly what's in it. If it's a graphics file that WordPerfect can read, you'll actually see the graphic itself. This is a really fast way to review what's in your graphics files. (If a file has both text and graphics in it, all you'll see is text.) You can find the document you're looking for without taking the time to open a new document window and clutter up your screen with a lot of windows.

The Viewer

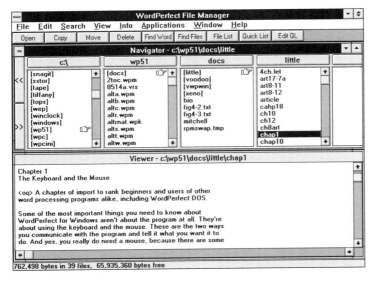

Viewer and text

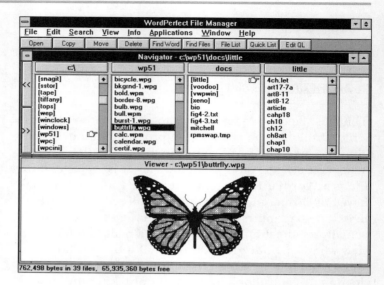

Viewer and graphic

Searching in the Viewer

Using the Viewer is a neat way to find exactly the document you're looking for without doing a complicated search. While you're looking at the document in the Viewer, you have access to WordPerfect's Search feature. Just press F2 to start a Viewer Search for the word or phrase you're looking for.

Say that you know the document you're looking for is probably Chapter1, Chapter2, or Chapter3, and the exact one you want has the phrase *exiting to DOS* in it. Click on the file's name to view it, press F2, put *exiting to DOS* in the Search box, and press Enter. If the phrase is in that document, you'll see it in the Viewer window. Press the Down arrow key to view the next listed chapter in the Navigator; then press F2 and Enter to search for the same thing again. Neat!

Selecting Files

You select files in the File Manager in the same ways as in Windows and WordPerfect, but with a few new twists.

- To select a file, just click on it.

- To select files that are next to each other, Shift-click: press and hold down the Shift key, click on the first one, and then click on the last one. Or drag over them; that will select them, too.

- To select files that aren't next to each other, Ctrl-click: press Ctrl and hold it down whole clicking on the files you want.

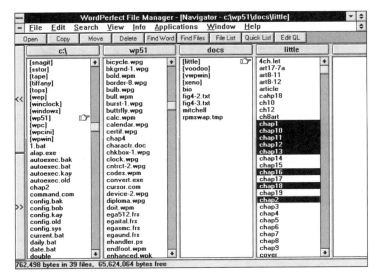

Selecting nonadjacent files

Deselecting Files

OK, you've selected a bunch of files, but there are a couple of them that you decide you don't want. Instead of selecting everything all over again, just deselect the ones you don't want.

- To deselect a file, press Ctrl and click on the file's name.

- To deselect *all but* one file, just click on that file.

Selecting in Different Directories

If you want to select files that are in different *directories,* use the File List. Just open a File List window for the different directories you want to select files from. Then you can Shift-click to select adjacent files, or Ctrl-click to select files that aren't next to each other. Once you've selected your files, you can use the Copy, Move, or Delete commands on them.

Selecting from different File Lists

Copying and Moving Files

Copying and moving files in the File Manager is a snap. It beats even the DOS 5 Shell. The easiest way is just to drag the files from one location to another in a File List window. You'll want to open the directory where the files are as well as open a File List window for the directory where you want to move or copy the files.

To move a file from one directory to another on the same disk, just drag it to its new location. To copy a file on the same disk, press Ctrl as you drag. *Moving* actually moves the file from where it is, but *copying* leaves the original alone and makes a new copy in the new location.

You'll see a little MOVE or COPY icon as you drag the file to its new location, and a dialog box will come up asking you to confirm that this is what you want to do.

If you'd rather fill out the To box instead of dragging files to their new locations, you can do that, too. Just select the files you want to move (copy, or delete) and click the Copy, Move, or Delete buttons. Or use the keyboard shortcuts Ctrl+C, Ctrl+M, or Ctrl+D. (Windows' F8 shortcut for Copy and F7 for Move don't seem to work here.)

If you're moving files from one disk to another, press Alt while you drag. This is a safeguard against your moving files from your hard disk to a floppy disk by mistake.

But if you're *copying* files from one disk to another, you don't have to press Ctrl. Confused? Here it is:

To copy onto a different disk	Drag
To move onto the same disk	Drag
To copy onto the same disk	Ctrl-drag
To move onto a different disk	Alt-drag

If you've selected more than one file, you'll get a somewhat different dialog box when you go to copy, move, or delete. You can choose Skip to skip any files that you've changed your mind about, or choose Copy All or Move All to do the whole operation at once.

Working with Several Files

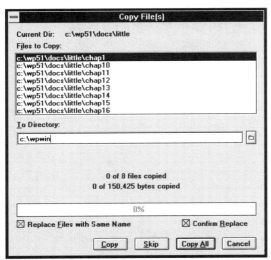

Using Wildcards

Another way to specify more than one file is to use wildcards. The characters * and ? are called wildcard characters. Just like in poker, a wild card can stand for something else. The asterisk represents any number of letters, and the question mark (?) represents any one character.

You can't use wildcards if you use the drag method of copying, deleting, and moving files. Instead, click the Copy, Move, or Delete button and enter the pattern for the file names you want to use.

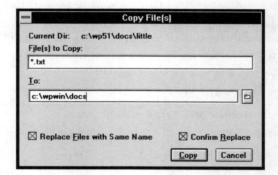

For example, to copy everything beginning with CHAP (like CHAP3 and CHAPT45), enter CHAP*. To copy everything beginning with A and having any extension, like APRIL.WRI or ABDOC.TXT or ACCOUNT.XLS, enter a*.*. To copy both the documents named BROWN and BRAUN, enter BR??N.TXT. Using wildcards can save you time, but they take a little getting used to. Entering *.*, for example, means "everything," so be careful with that one.

Renaming Files and Directories

You can also rename a file or a directory instead of really moving it from one place to another. Just give it a new name in the Move dialog box.

Customizing the File Manager's Windows

File List windows let you see detailed technical information about your files. Normally, their names, size, and date and time you last saved each one are shown, but there's a way that you can customize your File List. Click in the shaded part of the button bar. and a hidden pop-up menu will appear. You can choose Attributes to see a file's attributes (these are special tags that indicate to DOS whether a file's been used lately, whether it's a hidden file, and so forth), Full Path to see the full path name leading to where the file is stored, or Descriptive Name and Descriptive Type to have the File Manager search your document summaries and list the names and types you used there.

▶ **Tip:** *Click in the shaded part of the header, where the text buttons are, to use the hidden Column Manager in File List, Quick List, and Search Results windows.*

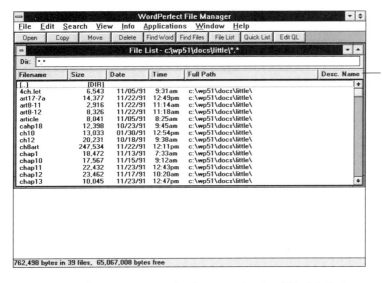

Click here for the Column Manager

You can also rearrange the buttons in the File List's button bar. Just drag them to where you want them. To remove a button (and the information that goes with it), drag the button out of the File List window. You can do this in Quick List and Search Results windows, too, but the buttons you can add will be different.

If the File Manager's windows are getting in your way, you can resize them. Move the mouse to the side of a window until it becomes a double arrowhead. Then drag it up and down or left and right to make the window larger or smaller.

There are also other ways that you can tell the File Manager to present your File List windows. Choose Options from the View menu, and you'll see this dialog box:

143

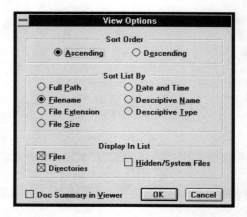

Here you can choose whether you want your file lists sorted by name (the standard way), by size, date modified, and so forth. If you like to see the files you worked with most recently at the top of your lists, click Date and Time under Sort List By.

One *more* thing you can do to customize File List windows (and Navigator windows, too) is change the font and font size used in them. Choose Font from the View menu and pick a new font and point size. You'll see a sample of what you get in the box underneath the list as you click on each font. Changing the font only works in the active window, so you have to do it one window at a time.

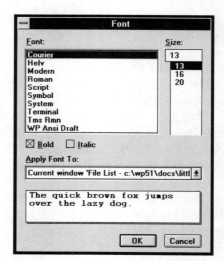

The File Manager is wonderful when it comes to finding things. You can search through your files for words are phrases, or you can search for file names and then, if you want to, search through them for words or phrases. An Advanced Find feature on the File Manager's File menu even lets you do very complex, sophisticated searches.

But simple searches are easy and fast. If you know that the document you're looking for has a special word or phrase in it, choose the Find Word button. Then enter the word or phrase you're looking for in the dialog box. You can use wildcards here, too, but it's better to use whole words or entire phrases so that the search results will be as close to what you're looking for as they can be.

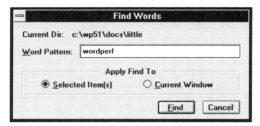

When the File Manager finds a document that has what you're looking for in it, he gives you a Search Results window and shows you the names of the documents he found. You can open a Viewer window to see right in the document where that word or phrase is! Now that's real service. If more than one document was located, they'll all be listed in the Search Results window, and you can click on each one to see what's in it.

Here's another neat trick. If the word or phrase is the one you're looking for, but it's not in the place you're looking for it, you can search through the document that's displayed in the Viewer window for the next occurrence of what you're looking for or something else by pressing F2, as you saw earlier. Say that the File Manager has found three documents that all contain *Lassie Come Home*. Now that you see which ones they are, you realize that the document you want also has *Elizabeth Taylor* in it.

Finding Things!

▶ **Tip:** *You can find files and words by clicking Options in an Open, Save, or Save As dialog box, too.*

Find Word

▶ **Tip:** *If you can select a few files to narrow the search before you start, that will speed things up.*

Search each one for Liz's name, and you've got it. This is how to do a complex search like the ones you can do with Advanced Find without having to learn the rules and figure out how to search for what you need.

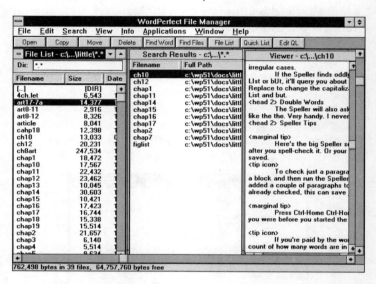

Customizing Search Results Windows

There's a hidden Column Manager in a Search Results window, too. You can drag the individual column buttons to new locations or get rid of some of them entirely just by dragging them off the button bar. Don't care about file sizes? Fine. Just drag the button away. You can get it back later by clicking in the shaded part of the bar. Clicking these shows you the new buttons that you can add, too.

Find Files

If you want to search for a specific file name or pattern of file names, click the Find Files button instead of the Find Word button. You'll get a dialog box where you can specify a pattern of file names to find. The pattern *.* will already be in the box, but change it to something else, because that *.* means "everything," and searching for that makes no sense.

But unlike the Find Word dialog box, it makes sense to use wildcards in the Find Files dialog, because of DOS's silly rules about using only eight characters plus a three-character extension for file names. They're so restricted and incomprehensible that patterns are easy to use. For example, you can find all the files that end in .TXT just by entering *.TXT.

When the File Manager finds the files you're after, you can use the Viewer to see what's in them, just as though you were searching for words inside them with the Find Word button. Here we searched for *ch**.

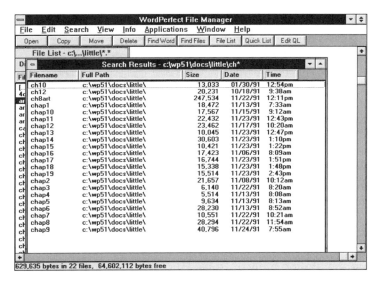

Searching by Date

We won't go into the Advanced Find features here except to say that you can use it easily to locate files that were created or changed on or after a certain date. Being able to search for date is very handy if you know that you worked on that document last Tuesday (maybe) but what on earth did you call it?

Choose Advanced Find from the Search menu, or press Ctrl+F2. Then, in the File Date Range boxes, enter the earliest date and latest date that you want to search through. For example, if you wanted to search through everything that's been saved since March 5, 1992, enter 03/05/92 in the From box and today's date in the To box.

147

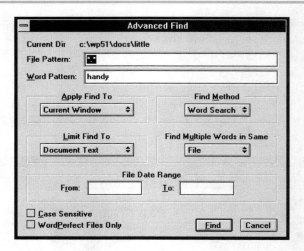

The File Manager will normally search through just the files that are listed in the active window. If you want to search your whole hard disk, use the Navigator to go back to your root directory—the one that has the c:\ above it. When that window's active, the search will look all over your hard disk.

File Manager Tricks

The File Manager has a few tricks up his sleeve that may not be immediately obvious. Here are some of them.

Minimize the File Manager

Remember, the File Manager is a standalone program. You can leave it in memory, ready to use whenever you need it. That's a lot faster than opening it from scratch every time you need it. So if you have the memory to spare, keep the File Manager handy by not closing it if you think you're going to go back to it later. You can just click on the border of a document that's peeking out around the edges to get back to WordPerfect proper, or you can minimize the File Manager by clicking on its Minimize icon. Once the File Manager's in memory, you can switch to it by choosing it from the Task List, which can be quickly brought up with Ctrl+Esc, or you can go out to the Windows desktop and click on the File Manager's icon, if you've minimized it. Personally, I think Ctrl+Esc is the fastest way because you don't have to shuffle through your windows.

The File Manager also has his own set of keyboard short-cuts, but mercifully they're easier to remember than some of WordPerfect's (and Windows'). Look at these:

Ctrl+P	Print
Ctrl+D	Delete
Ctrl+C	Copy
Ctrl+R	Rename
Ctrl+A	Attributes (change)
Ctrl+G	Change directory
Ctrl+T	Create directory
Ctrl+Q	Quick List
Ctrl+S	Select All
Ctrl+U	Unselect All
Ctrl+F	View File List
Ctrl+N	View Navigator

You can drag to select a bunch of files that are next to each other and then just choose Skip to skip copying or deleting those that you don't want. There'll be a Skip but-ton in the Copy and Delete dialog box.

Skipping Files

Want to copy, move, or delete everything in a directory? Highlight any one thing in the directory and then choose Select All (Ctrl+S is the keyboard shortcut).

Selecting All

It's often faster to Select All and then choose the files you don't want if there are only a few that you don't want. If there are a few files you don't want, skip them. Or Ctrl-click on the ones you don't want to deselect them before you start the copy, move, or delete operation.

These have been mentioned before, but here they are again, because they let you do neat tricks. You can move all of the File Manager's windows independently of each other. To resize one, drag it by a border. To rearrange its buttons, drag them (in File List, Quick List, and Search Results windows). To see if there are hidden new buttons you can add in these special windows, click in the shaded part of the window's button bar.

Window Tricks

All Sorts of Other Things

There are all kinds of other things you can do with the File Manager, but this is supposed to be a *little* book. So here are some of them, and you can explore the ones you're interested in:

- You can add programs to the File Manager's Applications menu so that you can start them from there without exiting from the File Manager and going to the Windows Program Manager. If you use spreadsheet or graphics programs with WordPerfect, you might want to be able to start them from the Applications menu, too.

- You can add buttons to the File Manager's button bar and rearrange or edit the buttons that are already there.

- You can get information about your system (such as the version of DOS you're running), about Windows, about your hard disk and floppy disks, about your printer, and so forth. Choose Info from the main menu.

- You can print documents from File List, Navigator, or Search Results windows. If the document you're printing was created in WordPerfect, it'll open in WordPerfect and then go to the printer that's currently selected. If you've chosen a non-WordPerfect document to print, it'll be sent to the Windows printer (yes, there is "WordPerfect printing" and there is "Windows printing"; see Chapter 11). The Printer Setup command on the File Manager's File menu doesn't let you switch printers; it just prints with the currently selected printer.

- You can print the contents of File Manager windows (which is useful if you want to create tiny directory listing that you can use as labels on floppy disks) or even copy the contents of File Manager windows to the Clipboard so that you can use them as graphics in your documents.

- You can copy or append selected text from the Viewer to the Clipboard.

- You can use the File Manager's own Preferences menu to tell it how you want to be prompted about things like printing and retrieving files. (It's on the File menu.)

- You can associate files with programs that can open them. If you've used Windows much, you're probably already aware of this technique. Once a file's associated with a program that can open it, all you have to do is double-click on the file's name to start the program running. The File Manager has a built-in Associate dialog box that's really easy to use. Choose Preferences from the File menu; then choose Associate. You'll be able to pick just about every type of file created by every

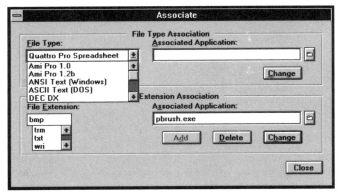

different program.

You can open other programs ("applications") and their documents through the File Manager (in the File List, Navigator, and Search Results windows).

- You can edit your Quick List in the File Manager to keep it up to date with the files you want quick access to.

- If you're used to WordPerfect for DOS's Long Document Names feature that you can use with document summaries, you can find it here in the File Manager, too. In the File List window, click in the shaded part. Then choose Document Name. The File Manager will scan all your document summaries and put the long document names in the File List window.

Take a few minutes to explore the File Manager. You'll be glad you did.

Love that File Manager

Spelling

Let WordPerfect correct your mistakes for you!

WordPerfect's Speller is great. I'm a terrible typist, so I just type away and then let the Speller correct everything for me. It usually knows what word I meant to type.

The Thesaurus is really useful, too, when you've over-worked a word and need to find another that means the same thing, or the opposite.

And if you justify your text or if you're finicky about hyphenation, you can use WordPerfect's hyphenation features to break words and the ends of lines just as you'd like. The program normally doesn't hyphenate words, but you can turn on hyphenation to tell it to use the hyphenation rules that are in the Speller's main dictionary.

The Speller

To run the Speller on a document, click on the Speller button (or choose Speller from the Tools menu, or press Ctrl+F1). Then click Start to start it going.

▶ **Tip:** *Spell-check a document before you print it, and save a tree.*

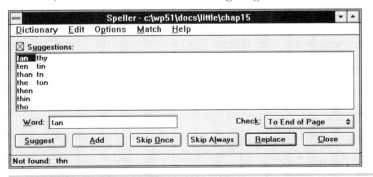

Normally, it's set to check your whole document, but you don't have to check the whole thing, and sometimes it's faster not to.

Checking a Page

If you just want to check the page the cursor's on, choose Page. If you've only made corrections on the current page, this is a lot faster than checking your whole document again.

You can also choose To End of Page to check just to the end of the page.

Checking a Document

To check the whole document, choose Document, or leave it as the choice, since it's usually already chosen. You can be anywhere in your document; you don't have to go to the top first.

Choose To End of Document to check just from where the insertion point is to the end.

Checking a Word

▶ **Tip:** *You can select text and just check the spelling in the selection. If you've just added a couple of paragraphs to a document you've already checked, this can save you some time.*

Sometimes a word that you've typed just doesn't look right, but you don't have to check the whole page to find out. To see if a word you've typed is spelled right, put the insertion point in the word and choose Word from the Check: pop-up list; then press Enter. You can click back in your document to pick a word even though the Speller window's open. If the word's OK, you'll see a "word found" message at the bottom of the Speller window. If it's not OK, you'll see a list of suggested alternates.

Choosing the Right Word

Once the Speller's found a word that it thinks is misspelled, it gives you all the words it can think of that are even close to the word you typed. Just double-click on the right word or press Enter if the right word's highlighted.

If you want to correct a word manually, double-click the word in the Word box; then just type the new word and press Enter. Or click back in your document and edit it there. Double-clicking on it to select it in the document and then retyping it is often faster than anything else, especially if it's really botched up.

If you want to allow the irregular spelling of a word just one time, click Skip Once. If you choose Skip Always, the speller skips that word for the rest of the spell-checking, not really for "always." If what you really want is to add that word to the dictionary so that it *will* always be skipped, choose Add.

The Edit options don't apply to editing a misspelled word, as you may recall from WordPerfect DOS. Here in WordPerfect for Windows, the Edit options apply just to the text in the Word box. You can cut, copy, and paste text from other programs into the Word box, and you can Undo the last change you made, too.

The Edit Options

The Speller normally stops if it runs across words with numbers, like F7. If you do a lot of typing with words like this, uncheck the Words with Numbers option on the Speller's Options menu so that you won't be bothered.

Speller Options

It also checks for duplicate words like *the the*. Very handy. I never see those. You can turn that feature off, too, by using the Options menu.

If the Speller finds oddly capitalized words like LIst or bUt, it'll query you about them, too. If you type a lot of acronyms or words that have odd capitalization, you may want to turn off checking for irregular capitalization.

Choose Replace to change the capitalization to normal, like List and but.

Here's the big Speller secret: **save your document after you spell-check it.** Or your changes won't be saved.

Getting the Most from the Speller

You can speed up the Speller by unchecking the Suggestions box. You may find it faster to just manually edit typos as the Speller locates them instead of letting it suggest a lot of words for you.

Also, you can work back and forth between the Speller window and your document, so feel free to edit text and then click Resume in the Speller window to keep on spell-checking. Pressing Enter also starts the Speller rolling again if you've stopped it by clicking back in your document.

The Speller is a separate program, so you can keep it handily in memory if you're going to want to get it back again quickly. Instead of clicking on Close to close the Speller, minimize it. First, make the WordPerfect window medium size by clicking on its double-arrow Minimize icon. Then minimize the open Speller window. With

WordPerfect less than full screen size (if you're not running anything else), you can see the icons of the programs you've minimized around the edge of your desktop.

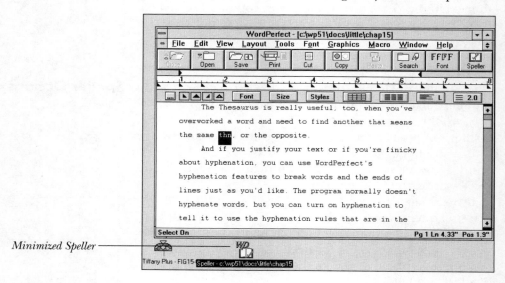

Minimized Speller

The Thesaurus

▶ **Tip:** *Keyboard shortcut:*
Alt+F1

If you can't think of the right word to use, try the Thesaurus. Put the cursor on a word you want to find a substitute for and then choose Thesaurus from the Tools menu (Alt+F1 is its shortcut). If WordPerfect has alternate words in its dictionaries, it will suggest them. If you see one you like, click on it and choose Replace. Double-click on a word that has a bullet next to it to see more suggestions that are related to it. You can look through a whole chain of synonyms and antonyms that way.

▶ **Tip:** *The Thesaurus's History menu keeps a list of the last words you looked up.*

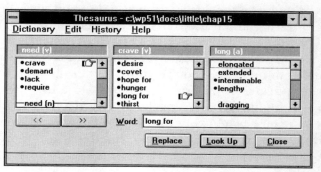

An (n) next to a word means that it's a noun. An (a) indicates an adjective, (v) is for verb, and (ant) is for antonym, or the opposite.

To go back into your document so that you can get a sense of the context you used the word in, just click back in your document. You can edit the document, too, and just click back in the Thesaurus when you're ready to use it again. Like the Speller, it can be minimized so that it's kept in memory, ready to go when you need it.

> **Tip:** *Minimize the Thesaurus when you first start it if you want to keep it in memory.*

Looking Up a Word Not in the Document

You can also look up a word that's not in your document. Type the word in the Word box (or paste one in through the Clipboard) and then choose Look Up.

Hyphenation

Normally WordPerfect doesn't break words at the end of a line. If you're justifying text, though, you may want to turn hyphenation on so that the word spacing in your document will look better.

To turn on hyphenation, select Line from the Layout menu; then select Hyphenation and OK.

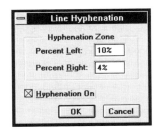

> **Tip:** *Go to the beginning of your document if you want hyphenation on in the whole document.*

From then on, if a word needs to be broken at the end of a line, WordPerfect will either hyphenate it or beep at you and ask you to hyphenate it, if it can't find the word in its dictionary.

You can hyphenate just part of a document, too. For example, if you're typing tables or using narrow columns, you'll probably not want to use hyphenation in them. (You'll get too many word breaks if you do.) To turn hyphenation off, position the cursor where you want to turn it off and then choose Layout, Line, and Hyphenation Off. You can turn it back on again after the table or columns.

Styles

16

Styles are in style.

Instead of formatting text as you're typing, you can apply styles to a document after it's typed. Not only can this save you a lot of time, but it's also especially handy if you change your mind about how your document should look. Instead of finding all your headings and changing them one by one, for example, you can simply change their **style.**

A style is just a combination of formatting codes that you can apply anywhere in your document. To change the formatting that's being used, you change the codes that make up the style.

In addition to formatting codes, styles can have font change codes, appearance changes like italics and small caps, size changes, and even graphics (how about a butterfly next to each main heading?) Here's how to create styles of your own.

Defining Your Own Styles

Chapter 8, "The Ruler Bar," showed how to use styles in your document by choosing them from the ruler's Styles button. Here you'll see how to set up styles of your own and save them.

Setting up a Style

To set up a style of your own, double-click on the Styles button. You'll see the Styles dialog box. Choose Create to start creating your own style.

```
┌─────────────────────────────────────────┐
│ ▭          Style Properties              │
├─────────────────────────────────────────┤
│ Name:                                    │
│ ┌─────────────────────────────────────┐ │
│ │ Heading 1                           │ │
│ └─────────────────────────────────────┘ │
│ Description:                             │
│ ┌─────────────────────────────────────┐ │
│ │ Head 1 for Brochures                │ │
│ └─────────────────────────────────────┘ │
│                                          │
│      Type          Enter Key Inserts     │
│  ┌──────────┐    ┌──────────────────┐    │
│  │ Paired ⬍ │    │ Hard Return    ⬍ │    │
│  └──────────┘    └──────────────────┘    │
│                                          │
│                  ┌────────┐ ┌────────┐   │
│                  │   OK   │ │ Cancel │   │
│                  └────────┘ └────────┘   │
└─────────────────────────────────────────┘
```

Enter a descriptive name in the Name box. You don't have to follow DOS's file-naming rules here, so use something that tells you what the style is, like Heading 1.

In the Description box, you can be even more descriptive and explain what the style is for, such as Head 1 for Brochures (you can only display about 20 characters).

Types of Styles

Type of style and Enter Key Inserts need a little explaining. Most of the time, the styles you create will be **paired** styles: the codes you use are turned on and then turned off at the end of the text you apply them to. For example, if you set up a style that uses boldface and 14-point type, only the text you use the style on will be 14-point bold.

There's also a type of style called an **open** style, though, and once it's turned on, it's not turned off again. Use open styles only for settings that you want to affect an entire document, like justification, line spacing, margins, and such.

Now the Enter key stuff. Normally, pressing the Enter key inserts a hard return in your document. But as far as styles are concerned, there's a neat thing you can do with the Enter key: you can have it turn the style off when you press Enter. If you're setting up a style for a heading, choose Style Off from the pop-up list under Enter Key Inserts. That way, as soon as you press Enter, the style's turned off and you can go on typing normal text.

If you're setting up a style that creates bullet lists or numbered paragraphs, you can choose Style On/Off instead. That way, as you type, the style's turned off and then on again when you press Enter to create the next bullet list item or paragraph.

When you've got the name and the description and the rest of this figured out, click OK. You'll get the Style Editor, where you can create the format codes that determine the style.

There's one thing that's hard to figure out about this window unless you've created styles in WordPerfect before, and that's the mysterious *comment*. But once you realize what it is, it's easy: *The comment represents the text that you're going to apply the style to.* So you put the codes that turn the style on before the comment. All you have to do is what you would normally do to create the formatting you want: *Press the keys or make the menu choices that generate the codes you want the style to have.*

Here's an example. Say you want to create a heading style that uses 14-point Helvetica bold type and has one blank line both above and below it. Press Enter, double-click on the Font button, and select Helvetica 14 point bold (you may have to select Bold from the Appearance box if you don't have a separate Helvetica Bold font); then click OK and press Enter again. Your screen should look somewhat like this one:

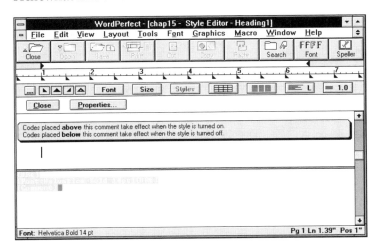

▶ **Tip:** *You don't have to turn off style changes at the end of a style, like changing back from bold text to normal; WordPerfect does that automatically when it turns the style off.*

When you click Close, your new style is added to the Styles dialog box. To see how to use it in a document, look back at Chapter 8 for tips on applying styles from the ruler.

Editing Styles   Another nice thing about styles is that you can edit them, and all the text that you've applied the style to will change as well. You don't have to go back through your document and change each and every occurrence of a first-level heading to something else, for example. All you need to do to edit a style is double-click on the Styles button, pick the style you want to change, click Edit, and change the codes to whatever you like. WordPerfect will reformat your document when you return to it. This is the real time-saving aspect of styles: you can reformat your document instantly!

Save Your Styles!   If you don't save a style that you've created in a style file, it will only be available in the document you created it in. If you want to use it in other documents, double-click on the Styles button in the Ruler, choose Save As from the dialog box, and save the styles you've created in a style file with a name that helps you remember it, such as brochure.sty. (It's a good idea to use the .sty extension so that you can identify a style file to use the styles that are in it later.)

Once you've saved a style file, you can retrieve it by double-clicking on the Styles button, clicking Retrieve, and choosing the style file's name.

Creating Styles by Example   Instead of manually entering codes for a style, there's a much faster way: You can just select text that's already formatted as you'd like it (be sure to include all the codes that control it) and then create the style.

Outline Styles   There's one other kind of style in WordPerfect, and it's called an outline style. You don't use the Styles button to create outline styles, though. Instead, you create them by using the Tools menu, choosing Outline, and choosing Define.

If you work with outlines a lot, you may want to create styles for them, such as switching to a different font or a different-sized font. Outline styles are also good for numbered headings in a document, or for numbered paragraphs.

Creating an outline style is like creating a regular style, except that you can specify a different style for each level of outlining you're using (1 through 8).

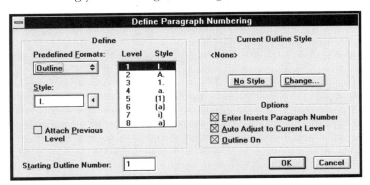

You can use (or edit) one of the predefined outline styles—Document or Technical Document—for the headings in a document, if you're using numbered headings. The Document outline style uses Roman numerals; the Technical style uses 1., 1.1, 1.1.1, and so forth. Test them out and see if you like them before creating an outline style on your own.

Applying Outline Styles

To use an outline style, choose Outline from the Tools menu; then choose Define (or press the keyboard shortcut Alt+Shift+F5). Choose Change to get to the Outline Styles list; then select the style you want to use.

Then, each time you press Enter, you'll get a numbered paragraph in the style you've chosen, with an outline number at the cursor's position. To go to a lower level, press Tab; to go back up a level, press Shift-Tab.

To turn off outline mode so that pressing Enter doesn't generate a paragraph number, choose Outline Off from the Tools Outline menu.

Make a Button for Outline Styles

All this is a little cumbersome, so my recommendation is that you make buttons for turning outline mode on and off, and applying whatever outline style you like, too, by recording macros. See Chapter 7, "The Fabulous Button Bar," for how to create a button of your own.

Graphics

17

How did you live without this before?

You probably bought WordPerfect for Windows for its superior graphics ability. Well, here it is. Graphics are surprisingly easy to use in WordPerfect for Windows, and you see on the screen what you'll get in your document (that is, unless you're in draft mode for speed). To move or resize a graphic image, all you have to do is drag it with the mouse. Text will automatically wrap around your graphics, even in columns.

Putting a Graphic in a Document

To bring a graphic image into a document, choose Figure and Retrieve from the Graphics menu. (Actually, you can bring a graphic image into any type of graphics box, but let's keep it simple here. You'll hear about this little mystery later in the chapter.) Then type the file name of the graphic image you want to use, including its path, if necessary, or double-click on a graphic's name to bring it into your document.

▶ **Tip:** *Shortcut for retrieving a graphic into a Figure box: press F11.*

WordPerfect graphics all have the extension .wpg, but you can use lots of other types of graphs, like TIFF files and EPS files and spreadsheet graphs (PIC files) and graphics you create in painting programs, like PCX files.

By the way, if you want to see all the graphics that came with WordPerfect, now is a good time to preview them. Highlight the first .wpg file and choose View. You can then press the down arrow key to see all the rest of them, one by one, in the View window.

▶ **Tip:** *You can also bring graphics into WordPerfect from another program through the Clipboard.*

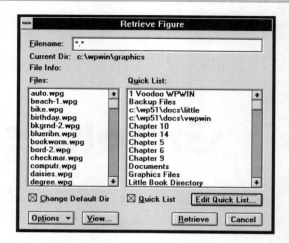

That's it. The graphic image will appear in your document, and you can drag it to move it, or click on it and put the cursor on one of its corners and push it in to make it smaller, or pull it out to make it larger.

The Figure Editor

▶ **Tip:** *Double-click on a figure to open the Figure Editor. Shift+F11 will let you use the Figure Editor, too.*

If you'd rather specify an exact size for the graphic and fine-tune it in a bunch of different ways to get special effects, don't just click once: *double*-click on the image. That will open the Figure Editor.

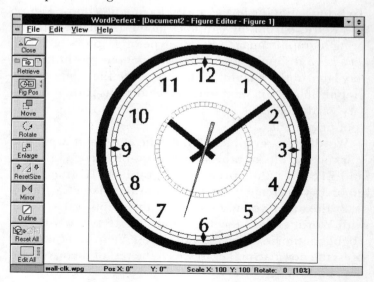

The Figure Editor has its own menu and button bar. On the Edit menu, for example, you'll see Move, Rotate, Scale, and things like that, instead of the familiar Cut, Paste, and Copy commands. We'll look at what these do in just a minute.

The View menu applies just to the Figure Editor's button bar. If you like lots of buttons, click on Button Bar Setup and choose Text only. That will make room for more buttons on the screen (you can add all sorts of buttons to the button bar by choosing Edit). If you'd rather have the button bar at the top or bottom of the screen instead of on the left side, you can choose another position for it.

▶ **Tip:** *You can edit the Figure Editor's button bar just like any other button bar, so put your favorite macros on it.*

Editing Graphics

Once you've got a graphic image in the Figure Editor, you can do all sorts of things with it. The button bar's buttons obviously let you retrieve a different graphic and close the Figure Editor (you can't switch to another document while you're in the Figure Editor), but the others may need a little explaining.

Fig Pos

To change the box's position on the page, you can use the Fig Pos button, or you can drag the box.

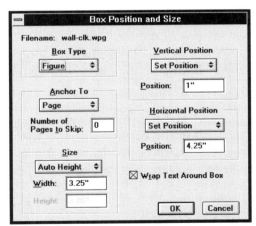

You can enter a specific position from the right margin, a vertical and/or horizontal position, and so forth. *This is also where you specify whether text is to wrap around graphics or not.* But be warned that if you don't wrap text around graphics, graphics and text can overlap. You may need to add space for the graphic by pressing Enter.

Anchor To lets you determine whether the graphic moves with the text that's all around it (Paragraph), stays at a fixed position on the page (Page), or is treated just like a character in a line (Character). The preset choice is for graphics to stay on the page, just where you place it, and text will (normally) flow around it, changing as you edit the text. With the Page choice, you'll also see a mystifying "Number of pages to skip." Leave it 0 if you want the graphic to stay on the current page, enter 1 to put it on the next page, and so forth.

If you choose the Character setting, the box will stay with the text character that's next to it, on the left. The consequence of this is that if you allow text to be wrapped, the line after that will start *underneath* the graphics box.

With the Paragraph type, the graphics box will stay with its paragraph, even if the paragraph moves to another location. Choose this type if you're wrapping text around a graphic and you want the graphic to stay with the wrapped text.

The anchor types affect how you can specify a graphic's vertical and horizontal positions on the page. For example, if your graphics box has a Paragraph anchor type, you can specify an offset of 0 in the Vertical Position box so that it will align with the top of the paragraph. If it's a Page-type anchor, you can choose Top or Bottom to align it with the top or bottom of the page. You can really get in here and fine-tune things.

> **Tip:** *Pressing Esc will close the Figure Editor without saving any of the changes you've made. Clicking the Close button makes the changes.*

Move The Move button lets you change the graphic image's position and size within the box, not the box itself. You use the arrow keys to reposition the figure in the box, or drag it with the mouse.

Rotate The Rotate button lets you rotate your graphic image for special effects. Click on the indicator lines, and you'll see the graphic rotate. Clicking on the horizontal axis line will rotate the image 90 degrees counterclockwise, and clicking on the left axis will turn it upside down (180 degrees). To position the graphic at another angle, click on the right axis.

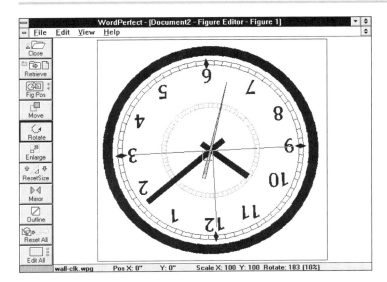

To enlarge or reduce a graphic image, click the Enlarge button. Drag the dotted line to create a box that's the size of the image you want.

Enlarge

To change the amount that a figure enlarges or reduces at a time, press the Ins key. Then look at the status bar in the lower-right corner of the screen. You can choose 25, 10, 5, or 1 percent. Once you've set a percentage, the image will grow or shrink by that percent when you press Ctrl+Up arrow or Ctrl+Down arrow.

You can also size an image in the document by clicking on it with the mouse and dragging one of the size boxes that appears inward or outward.

In addition, you can use the Scale command on the Figure Editor's Edit menu to reduce or enlarge an image by a set percent, the one that's showing on the status bar. Pressing Ins will change this percent, too.

This one lets you reset the size of the graphic to what it was before you began changing it to a different size. Very handy.

Reset Size

This button lets you switch the image to its mirror image ("opposite hand," as architects say). You can use it to get special effects in your graphics.

Mirror

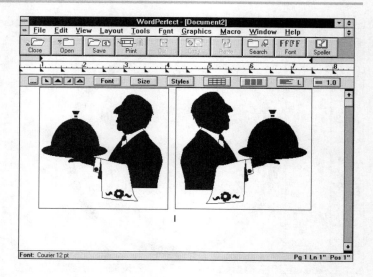

Outline The Outline button lets you switch to a pen-and-ink effect. Click the button again to get the graphic back to the way it was.

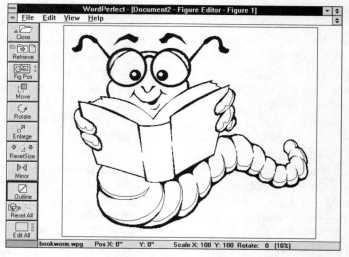

Edit All This handy button lets you do just about everything at once: move, scale, and rotate your graphic as well as switch to a mirror image, change to an outline, invert the image, and switch from color to black and white. If you want to try out a few different effects, use this button. It has a neat Apply box that lets you see the effects as you turn them on.

Edit All	
Move	**Scale**
Horizontal: 0"	Scale X: 100
Vertical: 0"	Scale Y: 100

☐ Mirror Image
☒ Outline
☐ Invert
☐ Black and White

Rotate
0

Apply   OK   Cancel

You can also do most of these things by using the Edit menu, but using the Edit All button lets you use that handy Apply box, too. (Drag the dialog box out of the way to see more of the figure!)

Reset All

Aha! The Reset All button is your Undo feature in the Figure Editor. You can click here to get things back to the way they were when you first started editing the figure.

Saving Graphics

If you want to save your edited graphic image as a separate image on disk, not part of the document you're creating it in, choose Graphic on Disk from the Figure Editor's File menu and give the graphic a new name. Don't use the original name unless you want to replace the original graphic with your newly edited one.

Getting Text in Graphics

Do you want to know how to put text in a graphics box? It's a little tricky. First, retrieve your graphic image; then click in the graphics box to select it. Now: press the right mouse button and choose Box Position. Select Horizontal and choose Margin, Full. Here's the essential part: uncheck the Wrap Text Around Box box and click OK. Now you can press Enter to move the insertion point into the box and type your text. Use Center Justification if you want it centered nicely.

▶ **Tip:** *Here's a neat trick for getting text in graphics.*

How did text
get in here?

More Things to Do with Graphics

In addition to creating special effects in your graphics with the Figure Editor, there are all sorts of other things that you can do with graphics boxes. For example, you can use captions, tweak the figure borders, and use shading in them.

Captions

If you want to use captions with your figures, use the Caption Editor. There's a trick for this. Click in the graphic with the right mouse button and choose Edit Caption (use the left mouse button to make your choice). You can then type a caption, use a different font for it, center it—format it just like any other line of text, in other words.

If you just want your figures numbered, such as Figure 1, Figure 2, and so on, open the Caption Editor and close it without typing anything. If you don't open it and close it, you won't get any figure numbering.

More Tricks

▶ **Tip:** *You can use this trick in the other kinds of graphics boxes, too.*

As you just saw, you can click the right mouse button on a figure to bring up the Graphics menu. But you can also click with the left mouse button in a figure to resize it or move it with the mouse. If you're moving it, be careful not to drag it by one of the "knobs" when the pointer's a two-headed arrowhead, or you'll resize it.

Graphics Options

You're not stuck with the preset formats WordPerfect uses for graphics boxes. Choose a type of graphics box from the Graphics menu; then select Options to see all the different things you can change.

▶ **Tip:** *Here's where you change figure borders and set up captions for Text boxes, Table boxes, Equation boxes, and so forth.*

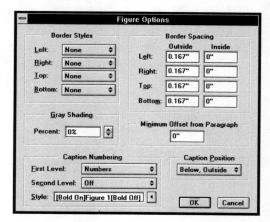

Most of these selections are pretty straightforward. For example, you can specify a position and size for the box, choose different border styles, and so forth.

Changes you make in the Options box affect all the figures of that type in your document from the insertion point on.

Deleting Graphics

Easy. Just click in the graphic and press Del or Backspace. You can delete the graphics box's code, too. It will say [Fig Box] or [Table Box] or whatever kind you're using. (You can search for these codes, too; see Chapter 13, "Finding Things.")

Graphics Boxes Demystified

One other thing that's a little "non-intuitive," as they say, about graphics is the different types of graphics boxes. There are five of them: Figure boxes, Text boxes, Equations, Table boxes, and "User-defined" boxes. *You can put anything in any of them.* The type of box you use just determines the preset options that go with it (but you can change them, too). For example, with a Figure box you get a single rule all around; with a Text box you get a heavy rule above and below, and shading inside; with a Table box you get heavy rules above and below, but no shading; and so forth.

> **Tip:** *To edit any kind of graphics box, double-click on it, and you'll be put in the editor for that type of box.*

If you put a graphic in a Figure box, you get to use the Figure Editor on it, and that's a plus if you plan to create special effects with the graphic. But you can use the graphics options to change the options for Figure boxes so that they look like Text boxes or Table boxes or whatever you like.

Table Boxes

Yes, you can put a table in a Table box. That way, you'll get to use WordPerfect's caption system that will keep track of table captions for you. But you still create the table by using the table icon in the ruler bar. Confused? The Table box is just another type of graphics box that you can put things in.

Text Boxes

Test boxes are great for text that you want to display in a document. They're often also called *sidebars* or *pull quotes* or *display quotes*.

> **Tip:** *Press Alt+F11 for a shortcut to create a Text box. Use Alt+Shift+F11 to edit one.*

You can put text in a text box and then move it and size it within a document for some nice special effects. For example, you can add gray shading to the box (but don't use much more than 10 percent if you want to be able to read what's in it), change the borders, and so forth.

To edit what's in a text box, double-click on the box, and you'll be put in the Text box editor.

Graphics Lines

You may know graphics lines as horizontal and vertical rules. No matter what you call them, they can give a professional effect to your documents.

To create a rule, choose Line from the Graphics menu; then pick Horizontal or Vertical.

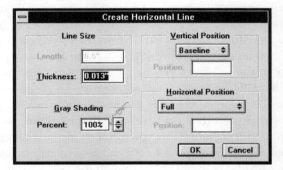

You can drag a graphics line to a new position on the page by using the mouse. Just click on it, and when the mouse pointer becomes a four-headed arrow, drag it to wherever you want.

If you drag a graphics line by one of the size boxes, you can resize it.

Use the dialog box to change the thickness of the lines for special effects.

Yes! There are keyboard shortcuts for these things, too. Ctrl+F11 is the shortcut for a horizontal rule, and Ctrl+Shift+F11 is the vertical rule keyboard shortcut.

More about Graphics

We've just scratched the surface of what you can do with graphics in WordPerfect for Windows. If you're interested in designing newsletters and brochures, you'll want to explore the program's graphics features further. Use Help. Experiment. What you see on the screen's pretty much what you get with graphics. Of course, the quality of graphics in your printed documents depends on your printer.

Linking

Magic. Change one document, and you change another.

WordPerfect for Windows lets you import spreadsheets (or parts of them) that you've created in other programs. But it doesn't stop there. It also lets you *link* documents to the original spreadsheet so that as you change the data in the spreadsheet program, the data in the WordPerfect document will also change.

You can import and link spreadsheets from PlanPerfect (WordPerfect Corporation's spreadsheet program), Lotus 1-2-3, Excel, Quattro, and Quattro Pro. New spreadsheets are being added all the time, so if the program you want to use isn't listed here, call WordPerfect Corporation to see if your favorite has been added.

There's another kind of like called a DDE link (for Dynamic Data Exchange) that lets you create a link to another Windows program while it's running. Its not quite the same as a spreadsheet link, but it has some of the same effects. You can edit the text, data, or graphics in the original program, and it will change in your WordPerfect documents, too. You'll see how to do this at the end of the chapter.

Importing and Linking a Spreadsheet

To import or link a spreadsheet, move the insertion point to where you want the spreadsheet to appear. Choose Spreadsheet from the Tools menu and then choose Import. Choose Create Link if you want to link it as well as bring it in. You'll see a dialog box where you can specify a range of cells to bring in instead of importing the whole thing.

```
┌─────────────────────────────────────────────────────────────┐
│ ▬              Create Spreadsheet Link                         │
├───────────────────────────────────────────────────────────────┤
│ Filename:   c:\qpro\sample.wq1                          [□]   │
│                                                               │
│ Range:   [                 ]    Reference:                    │
│ Range Name:                                ┌───────────┐      │
│ ┌────────────────────────────────┐        │    Type   │      │
│ │                                 │        │           │      │
│ │                                 │        │ ◉ Table   │      │
│ │                                 │        │           │      │
│ │                                 │        │ ○ Text    │      │
│ │                                 │        └───────────┘      │
│ └────────────────────────────────┘                           │
│                                     [ OK ]   [ Cancel ]       │
└───────────────────────────────────────────────────────────────┘
```

If you're just importing, the dialog box will look a little different. You'll be able to choose whether you want to bring in the spreadsheet as a table or as text. WordPerfect will let you bring in as many as 32 columns if you choose Table, but only 20 columns if you choose Text.

▶ **Tip:** *If you just import a spreadsheet, you don't automatically create a link, too.*

If you don't remember the exact name of the spreadsheet you want to use, click on the tiny folder icon to get a File List dialog box.

Click in the Range box to specify a range, such as A10:G20 or A10..G20 for cells in column A, row 10 through column G, row 20, if you haven't used named ranges in your spreadsheet. The program will display the size of the whole spreadsheet for you, but you probably don't want to use all of it.

If you select Text to bring the spreadsheet in as text, you'll get data in columns that are separated by tabs and rows that are separated by hard returns. Any heads that you centered in the spreadsheet program will become left-aligned. Also, you'll only get 20 columns of data per page. If you're bringing in data that you're going to want to format extensively in WordPerfect (add heads, change fonts, use boldface, and so forth), it's a better bet to bring it in as a table so that you can use the table editor that's built into the ruler on it.

If you select Table, WordPerfect will bring the spreadsheet data in as a table, just as it appears in the spreadsheet program. However, most spreadsheets are a lot wider than a regular WordPerfect page. If it won't all fit on a page, all you'll see is what will fit, and you'll get a warning that it extends beyond the document margins. Here are a few tricks you can use to make it fit:

• Go into the spreadsheet program and narrow the columns

• Change to a smaller font in WordPerfect

• Reduce the left and right margins in WordPerfect

• Bring in data in smaller chunks. For example, instead of importing data for September through December, bring it in a month at a time and label each table

• Print your table in Landscape mode (sideways).

You can also create a table structure first (see Chapter 8, "The Ruler Bar") and then import or link your spreadsheet. That way, it will appear just as you intend it to. If there are more cells in the data that's brought in than there are in your table, though, you won't get those cells. So check your spreadsheet first to see how big the range you want to use is.

When you bring the data in (I'm assuming that you linked it instead of just importing it), you'll see a "Link" and "End Link" notation in your document, above and below the spreadsheet data (it won't be printed in your final document, though):

DAY OF WEEK	DATE	LOCATION	TRANSPORT	HOTEL	ENTERTA
SUNDAY	06/18	SAN DIEGO	$89.00	$0.00	$10
MONDAY	06/19	SAN DIEGO	$9.00	$67.00	$32
TUESDAY	06/20	SAN DIEGO	$27.55	$67.00	$0
WEDNESDAY	06/21	SAN DIEGO	$12.50	$67.00	$98
THURSDAY	06/22	SAN DIEGO	$0.00	$67.00	$0
FRIDAY	06/23	SAN DIEGO	$0.00	$67.00	$0
SATURDAY	06/24	SAN JOSE	$133.00	$67.00	$0
TOTAL			$271.05	$402.00	$140

Editing Spreadsheet Tables

Once you've got the spreadsheet in as a table, you can double-click on any table column marker (above the ruler) to display the Table Options dialog box and fix up your table.

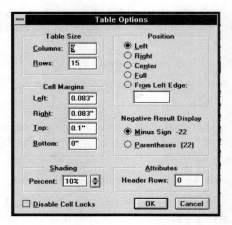

DDE

Spreadsheet links let you link just spreadsheet data, but DDE (Dynamic Data Exchange) links let you link just about anything—text, tables, graphs, what have you. The catch is that the other program has to be a Windows program that supports DDE, too.

Say, for example, that your art department's working on a complicated graphic. (If you're like me, *you* may be your art department, but you may be in a big company, working on a network.) You need to get the graphic in a document now, to hold a place while it's being fine-tuned (becauseif a committee's reviewing it, you know you won't see it "tomorrow"). With DDE, you can put the graphic in your document and link it to the original graphic in the program that's being used to create it. As the graphic changes, it will change in your document, too.

To do this, put the insertion point where you want to create the link. Choose Link from the Edit menu; then choose Create. Pick the program and the file that has the data you want to link and type a name for the link, something that helps you remember what it is.

▶ **Tip:** *You can make a Paste Link instead of a DDE Link. Open both programs and copy the data you want to link to the Clipboard. Then choose Paste Link instead. This pastes the contents of the Clipboard and sets up the link, too.*

You can then pick whether you want automatic or manual updating (with manual updating, the link is checked and the data is updated only when you tell the program to do it) and choose whether the data is text or graphics.

There are a couple of tricks you should be aware of when you make a DDE link. First, both the original document and the WordPerfect document have to be open so that they can communicate. If you open a WordPerfect document that has a DDE link in it, go out to the other program, open the document that contains the original linked material, go back to WordPerfect, and choose Link and Update from the Edit menu. The second trick is that the data you bring in will be formatted like it is in the original application (the other program). So if that's not how you want it to be formatted in your document, put the WordPerfect formatting codes that will format it your way before the [DDE Link Begin] code.

More and more programs are adding this capability. If you're part of a work group where a document is being created by several different individuals or teams at once, you're going to love it.

Macros

If you can do it once, you can make a macro to do it for you always.

Using macros is an almost magical way to get WordPerfect to do your work for you. Let's put it this way: if you can do it in WordPerfect, you can make it into a macro that will do it automatically. Think of the possibilities. You can use macros to

- Create your letterhead

- Type boilerplate text

- Set up a document format

- Search for something and change it to something else, or copy it or cut it and paste it in another document

- Create lists for you.

You can even use WordPerfect's sophisticated macro command language to carry out very complex tasks, like creating on-screen tutorials for others. But we won't get into that here; the macros in this chapter will be easy ones. After all, the macros you'll use most are the ones that do things that you do every day.

In its simplest form, WordPerfect's macro recorder just records exactly what you do as you carry out a procedure. If you make a mistake, that's OK: just correct it, and the macro will record the correction, too. (You can edit macros just as if they were documents, but we won't get into that, either.)

So feel free to experiment with macros. Once you've recorded one, you can put it on the Macro menu or make a button for it, so it'll be really easy to use.

Recording a Macro

To record a macro, choose Record from the Macro menu (or use the keyboard shortcut Ctrl+F10). Fill out the dialog box with a file name (follow DOS rules: only eight characters, and either use the extension .wcm or use no extension at all, and WordPerfect will add .wcm for you). Use a descriptive name that helps you remember what the macro does. In the optional Abstract box, you can make notes about how the macro's supposed to be used, like "Use for formatting all Petersen reports" or "turn on double spacing before using this macro."

▶ **Tip:** *To start recording, just press Ctrl+F10.*

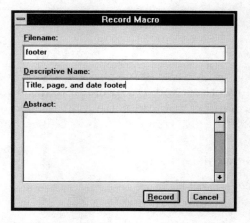

▶ **Tip:** *Don't use the mouse to position the insertion point when you record a macro. Why? Because that just records it relative to the current screen.*

Click Record to begin, and you'll see "recording macro" on the status bar. Everything you do—typing text, choosing from menus, using keyboard shortcuts, filling out dialog boxes—will be faithfully recorded until you choose Stop from the Macro menu or press Ctrl+Shift+F10.

A Sample Macro

For example, say that you want to set up a footer that contains a report title, the current page number, and the date, like this:

September Expenditures   Page 1   October 1, 1993

Here's how to do it.

Start the macro recorder running by choosing Record from the Macro menu or pressing Ctrl+F10. Name this macro, if you're following along, *footer*. Press Tab to move into the Descriptive name box and enter *Title, page, and date footer*. Press Enter to select Record.

Then choose Page from the Layout menu. Choose Footers and Create (leave Footer A selected). Then type *September Expenditures* (or the name of your report). Choose Center from the Layout Line menu or press Shift+F7. Then type *Page*, type a space, and click Page Number. Choose Line from the Layout menu and choose Flush Right. Pick Date from the Tools menu; then choose Date Text to get the date into your footer. Then click Close and stop recording the macro by selecting Stop from the Macro menu or pressing Ctrl+Shift+F10.

Now you've got a macro that creates a title, page number, and date footer. You can try it out by going to a new document and playing it. To see the footer, choose Print Preview from the File menu.

▶ **Tip:** *To change the text that's used in this macro, just open the macro (choose Open from the File menu and pick footer.wcm from the Macros directory) and change the text ("September Expenditures") to something else. Then save it, or Save it As another name with the .wcm extension, and you've got two macros.*

Playing a Macro

To run a macro that you've recorded, choose Play from the Macro menu or use the Alt+F10 keyboard shortcut. You can double-click on the macro's name to run it.

▶ **Tip:** *Keyboard shortcut: Alt+F10.*

A quick way to run a macro without reaching for the mouse is to press Tab to get into the list part of the dialog box; then type the first letter of the macro's name to move to it. When it's highlighted, press Enter.

Assigning a Macro to the Macro Menu

It's kind of cumbersome to use this dialog box for macros that you use a lot. You can assign your favorite macros to the macro menu so that you can choose them from there instead.

Choose Assign to Menu from the Macro menu; then click Insert and fill out the dialog box that you'll see with the macro's official file name and the name that you want to show up on the menu (keep it short). After you click all the OK boxes to get back to your document, there the macro will be, listed at the bottom of the macro menu.

Making a Macro into a Button

The Macro menu can fill up with your favorite macros right away. Instead of putting macros on the Macro menu, you can make them into buttons. This is really handy for macros that carry out specialized tasks, because you can put them on individual button bars that you use whenever you're doing that specialized task, whatever it may be. Suppose, for example, that you've created a button bar for doing mail merges. You could put a macro for formatting mailing labels as a button on the mail-merge button bar.

Ideas for Macros

Here are some things that you might like to record macros for. You'll undoubtedly think of others:

- A macro that creates your signature block and title
- Macros that change to different fonts and point sizes
- A macro that transposes words or sentences by cutting and pasting
- Macros that insert special characters, such as a paragraph symbol or infinity sign
- A macro that sets up a style for headings
- Macros for numbering paragraphs in different styles
- Macros for numbering pages in different formats
- Macros for creating the formats you use: a report, a business letter, a newsletter, whatever
- Macros for automatically creating tables of contents.

Entire books have been and are being written about WordPerfect macros. (In fact, I wrote one for WordPerfect DOS macros.) They're fascinating, and they certainly make your work a lot easier. But they're not necessarily "hard."

They *can* be hard, though. Those are the macros that use specialized macro command language, sort of like a programming language, to carry out complex sequences of instructions that you don't want to have to remember. But the best macros are the ones you use every day, the ones that just automate what you do all the time anyway.

If you're interested in exploring more sophisticated macros, the kind that you "program" instead of record, you should be aware that the macro language changed drastically between WordPerfect DOS and WordPerfect for Windows. If you have favorite WordPerfect DOS macros, they're not compatible with WordPerfect for Windows unless you convert them or rewrite them. But the good news is almost anything that can be done in WordPerfect for Windows has a corresponding macro command. In fact, there are over 600 macro commands that you can use. Obviously we can't go into them here, but you can order the special WordPerfect for Windows macros manual by calling 800/321-4566.

Index

A

active default printer, 116
active help, 24
Adobe Type Manager, 113
Advanced Find features, 147
aligning text, 66, 93, 94
alignment (justification), 73-74, 82
.ALL files, 115
alphanumeric words, checking, 155
anchor type, 168
annotating Help, 26
appending documents to each other, 21
appending to the Clipboard, 21
Applications menu, in File Manager, 150
applying styles, 68
arabic numbers, 88
arranging windows, 18-19
arrow keys, 4
assigning a symbol to a key, 123
associating files and programs, 151
attributes, 79
auto code placement, 75
automatically displaying the ruler, 63

B

background printing, 107
Backspace key, 3
backups, 37-38
bitmapped fonts, 112
.bk! extension, 38
Block Protect feature, 87
boldface, 79
bookmarks, in Help, 25
borders, of graphics boxes, 172
breaking a page, 86
bullet lists, 81
button bar, 12, 53-61, 124
buttons
    adding to File Manager, 150
    in File Manager, 143
    making macros into, 184

C

Cancel key, 4
canceling a dialog box, 33
capitalization
    changing, 81-82
    checking in Speller, 155
Caps Lock, 3
captions, using, 172
cartridge fonts, 114
cascading menus, 28
cascading windows, 18-19
center justification, 73
center tabs, 64

centering text, 73, 82, 91
changing margins, 66-67
character anchor, 168
check boxes, 30
clearing a document, 21
clearing tabs, 65
clicking, with mouse, 8
Clipboard
    appending to the, 21
    using the 98-99
clock, resetting your computer's, 46
closing a document, 21
codes, searching for, 126
color schemes, selecting, 40-41
colors
    in draft mode, 22, 39, 40
    in Reveal Codes, 15, 40
column margin marker, 69
columns, in tables, 69
columns, text, 71-72
command buttons, 31
Conditional End of Page command, 87
context-sensitive help, 23
Control icon, 17-18
Control Panel
    for installing Windows printer, 116
    to customize mouse, 8-9
controlling printing, 108-109

This *Little WordPerfect for Windows Book* was written in WordPerfect for Windows (of course) on a homebrew 386 clone, transferred over a TOPS/Sitka network to a Macintosh II (take that, DOS), and paged in Aldus PageMaker (thank you, Matt Kim). Screen shots were taken by Tiffany Plus from Anderson Consulting and Software of Bonneville, Washington. The fonts used are ITC New Baskerville and Futura Bold, both from Adobe Systems. The book's design, which includes custom Little Book fonts, is by Olav Martin Kvern, based on an original design by Robin Williams.

More from Peachpit Press. . .

DeskJet Unlimited, 2nd Edition
Steve Cummings
This is an in-depth guide to the HP DeskJet family of printers. It explains how to use these printers with major word processing, spreadsheet, graphics, and desktop publishing programs. Additionally, it includes extensive information on fonts (including downloading and converting from LaserJet format), troubleshooting, DeskJet programming, and tips on practical tasks such as printing envelopes and label sheets. *(428 pages)*

Desktop Publishing Secrets
Eckhardt, Weibel, and Nace
Here's a compilation of over 500 of the best tips from five years of *Publish* magazine. The tips cover all the major desktop publishing software and hardware products, including Ventura Publisher, PageMaker, WordPerfect, CorelDRAW, Windows, PostScript, fonts, laser printers, clip art, and more. *(536 pages)*

EcoLinking
Don Rittner
Eco-activism—using personal computers and modems to bring together the international environmental community—is just a keystroke away! *EcoLinking*, the first guide to this growing phenomenon, details how computer networks, bulletin boards, and online services can be put to work to save the planet. Giving step-by-step instructions, the book shows how to access the immense amount of environmental information found on worldwide computer networks. It also explains how to conduct online scientific and environmental research using bibliographic retrieval services, CD-ROM databases, and news services. Included are comprehensive appendices listing recommended communications software, describing "gateways" to the networks, and suggesting further reading. *(300 pages)*

The LaserJet Font Book
Katherine Pfeiffer
This book doubles as a buyer's guide to LaserJet fonts and a tutorial on using type effectively in your documents. Hundreds of LaserJet fonts from over a dozen vendors are displayed, accompanied by complete information on price, character sets, and design. The book includes scalable fonts for the LaserJet III printer, as well as bitmapped fonts used by the LaserJet II, IID and IIP printers. *(450 pages)*

Letter to a Computer Novice
Lawrence Magid
This book is an introduction to personal computers that assumes no prior technical knowledge. It demystifies computers and computerese, giving you the lowdown on hardware, software, buying and setting up a system, networks, and online services. *(160 pages, available 3/92)*

The Little DOS 5 Book
Kay Yarborough Nelson
Finally—all you need to know about DOS 5 is organized concisely and written in plain English. This book is packed with plenty of tips as well as an easy-to-use section on DOS commands. It also covers DOS basics, working with files and directories, disk management, and more. *(160 pages)*

The Little Laptop Book
Steve Cummings
Now you can get on the fast track to note–book and laptop computing. This book covers choosing a laptop, protecting it from theft and damage, hot tips on applications and utilities, printing on the road, and telecommunication. *(192 pages)*

The Little WordPerfect Book

Skye Lininger

Teach yourself the basics of WordPerfect 5.1 in less than an hour. This book shows you just enough to start creating simple letters, memos, and short reports—fast. Gives easy-to-understand, step-by-step instructions for setting page margins, typing text, navigating with the cursor keys, basic editing, printing, and online help. *(160 pages)*

The Little WordPerfect for Windows Book

Kay Yarborough Nelson

This book gives you the basic skills you need to create simple documents and get familiar with WordPerfect's new Windows interface. It also covers more advanced topics, such as formatting pages, working with blocks of text, using different fonts, and special features including WordPerfect's new mail merge, tables, equations, indexes, and footnotes. This book gives you hundreds of practical tips you can use every day condensed into one slim volume. *(160 pages)*

Mastering Corel Draw, 2nd Edition

Chris Dickman

This book—and its accompanying disk—provides beginning lessons and advanced tips and tricks on using CorelDRAW 2. Tutorials include manipulating shapes, grouping graphics, text shapes and paths, fills, and color. Appendices cover file exports, slide creation, and techniques for speeding up the program. A special color section displays award-winning drawings, along with tips from their creators. *(416 pages, plus disk)*

PageMaker 4: An Easy Desk Reference (PC Edition)

Robin Williams

This is a reference book, rather than a tutorial, organized to answer any PageMaker question as quickly as possible. Includes a tear-out shortcuts chart and an industrial-strength index. *(784 pages, available 3/92)*

PageMaker 4: Visual QuickStart Guide

Webster and Associates

This is a fast, highly visual, and highly inexpensive introduction to the leading page-layout program. With 300 illustrations in a short 160 pages, you learn by seeing. Section One leads you on a brief guided tour of the entire program; Section Two presents information by task; Section Three provides a reference of menu commands. *(160 pages)*

Ventura Tips and Tricks, 3rd Edition

Nace and Will-Harris

This book was described by Ventura President John Meyer as "the most complete reference for anyone serious enough about using Ventura." Packed with inside information: speed-up tips, special tricks for reviving a crashed chapter, ways to overcome memory limitations, etc. Features a directory of over 700 products and resources that enhance Ventura's performance. *(770 pages)*

Winning! The Awesome and Amazing Book of Windows Game Tips, Traps, and Sneaky Tricks

John Hedtke

This book gives you the inside story on the games in the Microsoft Entertainment Packs, as well as Solitaire and Reversi. It includes the complete rules and instructions for each game, as well as their hidden features. Finally, it shows some sneaky tricks learned directly from the games' programmers that let you rack up huge scores and super-fast times. Whether you're an occasional dabbler or a hopelessly irredeemable addict, this book will show you how to have even more fun with Windows.
(224 pages)

WordPerfect: Desktop Publishing in Style

Daniel Will-Harris

This popular guide to producing documents with WordPerfect 5.0 and 5.1 opens with a simple tutorial and proceeds through 20 sample documents, each complete with all keystroke instructions. Will-Harris covers the desktop publishing scene, from graphics programs to laser printers, fonts, and style sheets. If you're desktop publishing with WordPerfect, this book, as the *New York Times* put it, "could be a lifesaver."
(654 pages)

Order Form

(800) 283-9444 or (510) 548-4393
(510) 548-5991 fax

#	Title	Price	Total
	DeskJet Unlimited, 2nd Edition	23.95	
	Desktop Publishing Secrets	27.95	
	EcoLinking	18.95	
	The LaserJet Font Book	24.95	
	LaserJet IIP Essentials	21.95	
	Letter to a Computer Novice	12.95	
	The Little DOS 5 Book	12.95	
	The Little Laptop Book	14.95	
	The Little WordPerfect Book	12.95	
	The Little WordPerfect for Windows Book	12.95	
	Mastering Corel Draw, 2nd Edition (with disk)	32.95	
	PageMaker 4: An Easy Desk Reference (PC Edition)	29.95	
	PageMaker 4: Visual QuickStart Guide (PC Edition)	12.95	
	The PC is not a typewriter	9.95	
	Ventura Tips and Tricks, 3rd Edition	27.95	
	Winning! The Awesome and Amazing Book of Windows Game Tips, Traps, and Sneaky Tricks	14.95	
	WordPerfect: Desktop Publishing in Style, 2nd Edition	23.95	

Tax of 8.25% applies to California residents only. UPS ground shipping: $4 for first item, $1 each additional. UPS 2nd day air: $7 for first item, $2 each additional. Air mail to Canada: $6 for first item, $4 each additional. Air mail overseas: $14 each item.	Subtotal	
	8.25% Tax (CA only)	
	Shipping	
	TOTAL	

Name	
Company	
Address	
City State Zip	
Phone Fax	
❑ Check enclosed ❑ Visa ❑ MasterCard	
Company purchase order #	
Credit card # Expiration Date	

Peachpit Press, Inc. • 2414 Sixth Street • Berkeley, CA • 94710
Your satisfaction is guaranteed or your money will be cheerfully refunded!